Mud Lotus Mystic

The Poetry and the Practical, Methods of the Inner Journey

Cyrus Bruton

muswell hill press

London • New York

First published by Muswell Hill Press, London, 2017

British Library CIP Data available

ISBN: 978-1-908995-21-6

Printed in Great Britain

Dedicated to
Osho

Acknowledgements

I would here like to express my gratitude and acknowledge the following people who, together with their works, have directly or indirectly contributed to the birth of this book. Firstly Osho, Bhagwan Shree Rajneesh, who set me off on the path when I read his words forty years ago, saying that which I was feeling but could not articulate. Sri Ramana Maharshi, a beacon of light who goes on transmitting presence tangibly. Mikaire for being who he is, for his insistence on being to the point in action, and in whose presence I realised my true nature. To Isa Luerssen for her guidance and inspiration. Veeresh for his unconditional love and friendship. Christina and Stanislav Grof for developing Holotropic Breathwork, and the trainers for holding the space. Harry Palmer and the Avatar tools for sharing understanding. Hoffman Quadrinity teams for their work in a magical-mystical-therapy. My mother for opening the door, getting out of the way and then meeting me on the path. Annette for love, always being here and saying yes and no. The Berlin Sangha for receiving and persisting. To Jenny Cattermole for editing and staying with it when those sentences were mind bending. And finally to Tim Read and Mark Chaloner for bringing this book to the world.

Contents

Introduction

Does anybody read intros?

Lovers read intros. Lovers love the seasons. Perhaps at the beginning of being lovers we love the spring, but as love matures it deepens and winter becomes a rich, stripped-down, turned-in place of rest. The beloved doesn't age and love remains.

And that is how it is. If you turn up, a smile turns up and joy, life, gratitude and more all turn up, but first it requires you. That is what this book shares, different ways to get out of our own way and turn up as we naturally are. It is an invitation to our own re-source-full-ness, an invitation to become the spring of our own investigation, where our light and aliveness reveal the path, and this book, as with our path in life, does not move in a straight line.

The book is a collection of essays, meditation methods and poetry written mostly during breaks in a walk, a break in work, especially garden work, or after morning sitting meditation. There is something about the action of walking, the rhythm of the body in motion and the breath that for me brings about insight. I have always been attracted to methods and techniques and have enjoyed experiencing and observing in others how certain thoughts, words and actions brought together can spring the mind from its hold, bring us to the understanding that 'I have a mind but I am not the mind,' and return us to our original state, whether it be a glimpse or an irreversible shift. As the Indian mystic Kabir says, 'Wherever you are is the entry point.'

This book is biographical in the sense that the methods are particular to the path I have travelled, my own practice of living daily life and spending time with fellow travellers who inspired in me by their company a certain sharing of word and method. But the real sharing was before the word and thought, and perhaps these words can also act as catalysts, sending the reader back through words to the place before words and thought. Here in this book, the written word has its place exactly there, in the triggering and provoking of the only real knowing, which is being.

I love to read what speaks to me and I am grateful to all those writers. Each book I cherish has in it the voice that says, 'These words are not it,' whether the writer was aware of it or not. So as I am reading, the words disappear and the sense becomes my sense, because the sense of the writer merges with mine. And the only sense is that the words are not it, this is.

The words are not it, this is.

May this book contribute to the continuing deepening of this journey we are on together, through whatever situations we find our-selves in. It is my belief that, despite the great technological advance-ments of our recent past and approaching future, without the inner work and play and an understanding of who we truly are, our advancements will continue to be our destruction, because the mind we are operating through has remained the same. This book is dedi-cated to the dropping of the head into the heart and to the journey from mind to no-mind.

Cyrus

Berlin, January 2017

PART 1

Beginnings of a Path

Fragments

Fragments are all we are ever given and we remain fragmented when we stay with what we receive.

All thoughts, concepts and ideas are fragments. Even the idea of who we are is a fragment. An accumulation of thoughts which are fragments cannot be anything but a fragment – yes a big fragment, a pile of fragments, a net of fragments, with you jumping from one fragment to another. You, a fragment that has a preference for one fragment this moment and another fragment the next. But in reality each of us is the joining factor. These fragments cannot join themselves and we ourselves remain fragmented and separate when we continue to focus on and specialise in parts and never bring our attention to the whole. This is like believing the pictures on the cinema screen are the screen itself, when in reality the pictures are just the movement of light and shadows.

Knowingly or unknowingly, we are continually asking ourselves to be whole. This is the underlying prayer for peace or the attempt to make sense of the seeming differences. In Reality, we are that sense and we are that peace and we are the underlying nature of everything, but we do not *make* this sense and we cannot explain, measure or analyse it. I mean, how can you sense your self? If you could, you would have to be other than your self, and who would trust this other to verify who you are? And what sense would you use? Any sense would lead us back to fragmentation, so this sense must be something beyond the senses. But we do sense our self, who we are, and this sense is not of our making, because the sensing and the one who senses are one package. Whole.

It is called Being. It is this sense Being, which is not made, that makes sense and makes whole. Can you make Being? Okay you can pretend, but feel it, can you *make* Being? Can you *do* Being? No, because Being is first. It *is* already. You and I *are* already, we are already, all ready. Ready whole, ready to go, ready to stop, ready to do whatever you choose because Being includes all. It is who we are, this all-inclusive Being which reveals the wholeness. It is not a making or a doing. The makings and doings perpetuate the fragmentation, because we start doing to some-thing and our doing fragments it further in order to make it understandable, which always involves breaking it down and analysing it. Then each part needs to be broken down and analysed ad infinitum.

Have you ever had a disagreement with another person and noticed that each time we add another argument to prove our point the disagreement gets bigger? But when we shut up the atmosphere settles and, in that space, perhaps an agreement can be reached, but rarely in the heat of the argument.

Or have you ever tried to work something out and noticed that each thought just adds to the heap of thoughts that in turn you try to work out? Finally, when you leave it and give up, the mind settles and in that calmer climate understanding arises, but never in the heat and turbulence of the mind while you flail around trying to flush out the solution.

In my understanding this means that we do not stop at a fragment, no matter how great or impressive it appears. What we need to do when we receive something is to bring it completely into ourselves, feel it in all ways possible and allow a response, which is not considered or thought about, to arise. This feeling in all possible ways short-circuits the tendency of the mind to assert its known agenda and present its habitual solution.

The mind is not so strong, but we are, and it is only we who give power to the mind, so we can disconnect it by just breaking its habit, leaving a gap or, more accurately, becoming aware of the gap. Stop filling it with thinking and start feeling in more ways than we usually do. In this way, the response comes out of who we are, and then we start giving back, not repeating automatically or reacting but creating out of nothing. Oh, and by the way, it also makes for many interesting situations, because you yourself will be surprised at the responses. Each moment is new, a new you each moment.

D. H. Lawrence writes about this transformation through becoming nothing in the poem *New Heaven and Earth*:

V
God, but it is good to have died and been trodden out,
trodden to nought in sour, dead earth,

quite to nought,
absolutely to nothing
nothing
nothing
nothing.

For when it is quite, quite nothing, then it is everything.
When I am trodden quite out, quite, quite out,
every vestige gone, then I am here ...

Excerpt from *New Heaven and Earth* by D. H. Lawrence,
verse V (edited), from *The Complete Poems of D. H. Lawrence.*

The True Practice that Honours Life

If existence can adapt and respond to whatever happens then we,
being existential, also can. Strange that we think we need to prepare
and so create a somebody who needs to be prepared. Obviously that
somebody who is created thinking they need to be prepared already
believes that that which is existential in them cannot take care of life.
That is like the iceberg resisting melting because it has forgotten that
it is surrounded by itself and thinks that this thing in which it floats,
the ocean, will drown it if it melts. This somebody who is trying to
be prepared stands in the way of life like a foreign body, a stranger.
This stranger, by trying to do what is not their job, suffers in carrying
this burden. As most people think they are in control of their lives, or
should be, then each of these people is identifying with or thinking
they are this stranger and are in some way threatened by life. If we
can, with awareness, let life in in whatever form it comes to us and
let life out in whatever form it comes, then we will be existential,
responding as existence. That is the true practice of honouring life
and acting from integrity. This is not learned – this is life in life, life
that is whole in itself and naturally does not harm itself. It is life liv-
ing as you and I, and we do not cause each other or ourselves pain.

Stopping

Most people won't stop. They fear to stop because they believe
that stopping will be death. In a way, they are right: it will be

the death of the illusory search with its goals of improvement, change, or reaching something that would make the person into some-thing.

In stopping we are atomic: we are where the Big Bang has never stopped. That is, if you believe the Big Bang was the source of our universe, which is commonly accepted scientific knowledge these days. Or one could also say our birth has never stopped, and call this the Big Birth, where we are present at our death and birth simultaneously.

For the one who thinks they are some-body, stopping is like death because the some-body always needs to keep going to get some-thing and to add some-thing to fill out the some-body they think they are. When we stop, we naturally and effortlessly gather immense energy. All that energy which has been going into becoming somebody, being somebody and getting something is available to us.

Stopping is becoming aware of Being and the immense and unlimited energy of Being called existence. That is what I mean by atomic: it is one and indivisible. It does not need anything else to be what it is. As a person observes this phenomenon and brings their full attention to it, it grows. This growing can evoke fear because it seems to take over. In reality, it is not taking over but has always been here: this is life, and we are simply experiencing it fully. This is the re-enactment of the story in which the servants play at being the masters of the house while the real master is away. The fear that the servants have when they hear the sound of the master's car coming up the gravel driveway, after days of pretending to be the masters of the house, is the same fear of the one who believes they are the doer. As soon as the servants hear the car coming up the driveway they know who is in charge.

It is the life force on which everything we do is based. It is only our mistake to think that it is our doing when really the life force is the doer and goes on with or without us.

It is this life force which gives us this sense of being we call I AM. When I AM forgets this and defines itself through what is being done then the life force is forgotten as the prime mover.

The one who has defined himself as 'I am the doer' starts to believe he is independent of the life force. This forgetfulness contin-ues until we are brought back to remembrance through becoming conscious of our situation, exhaustion, realisation of approaching death, or whatever is needed to bring about Understanding.

Yes, we need to adopt this separate I. In fact, it is better to say we are this separate I. Understanding is knowing we are separate and connected to the whole at the same time and that we are not limited. After all, unlimitedness would have to be beyond separation and connectedness as each of these is just a varying degree of the other and hence a limitation. When we stop, we resume our original unlimited, immeasurable nature. We stop defining who we are and start being who we are and going with life.

The other strange thing is that in the forgetfulness we always plan, thinking we can get power and be immortal by dreaming great dreams into the future. But the power is here as life, and it is this which is immortal, unlimited and indestructible. So the illusory separate self has an upside-down view of life and misses from the first step because the first step steps away. The power to create and maintain all creations is here now and once this power is removed decay begins.

> Work, apart from devotion or love of God, is helpless and cannot stand alone.
> Sri Ramakrishna

> I am the vine, ye are the branches: He that abideth in me, and I in him, the same bringeth forth much fruit: for without me ye can do nothing.
> John 15:5

When that power or life force is no longer flowing into a body there is no sentience and the body decays. So who has the power? The body? You and I? Can we plan to live forever? No, but we can be that life which is forever, as Jesus spoke about many times. That is what is meant by heaven and nirvana: life eternal without the conditions of time. Nirvana actually means blowing out the candle, so our job is to blow ourselves out through burning bright. To see that we were never lit and we were never a separate light and then to go on as we really are. Burn without fuel, shine without source.

*

The seagull, like we humans, desires as it flies to do nothing, to stop and just hang in the moment. That is one of the highest arts of living.

One Look

Imagine walking through a space where there are obstructions randomly distributed like furniture and you intend to reach the door to go out. You navigate the obstructions as you continue to move towards the door and when you reach the door you step outside. As you had sight, you could see clearly all of the time. You navigated the space, changing direction when needed, but were never hindered in your progress towards the door.

Looking within we have an inner-sight to find our source. There is one direction, IN, and this inner place is close, intimately close. On the way we may meet the content of our mind in the form of thoughts and feelings, but unless we choose, through the habit of identification, there is no reason to stop looking within. This one look of in-sight is like the perfect downhill slalom skier. The gravity of source is drawing us in and our looking is so clear and total that even to see objects has a certain pleasure to it as it challenges us again and again, keeping us alert. We need to apply ourselves, to give ourselves, and each time we do we become more Self. As we look into space beyond the objects, we learn how to navigate, understanding that this infinite variety of objects need have no power over our attention and that it is only our forgetting to look in and be that hinders us. There is one direction and nothing to analyse or understand. One Look. In fact, inwardly, there is no need to navigate – we can follow the one direction and we only need to persist. Like clouds are these thoughts and there is no need to avoid them. We can pass right through them.

Awareness Is Our Treasure

Awareness is our treasure and as awareness we are aware of and at the centre of that which we experience. There is no need to attack thoughts and break into the mind to find the meaning or the treasure, as we are already inside, like the bank robber in the film, *The Inside Man*. We just need to realise our situation, then we permeate our mind from the inside. Free with mind and free without mind. Free in mind, using it and free outside of mind, aware of it.

Precious Life

For most people deprived of breath, the only motivation takes the form of 'How?' or, 'How to stay alive?' Then, when the breath is re-established, normal living is experienced and there is relief, some sort of 'Ah' associated with the gratitude and wonder of simply being. In the English language we don't have a punctuation mark for relief. We have a variety of punctuation marks, including exclamation and question marks, but no relief mark – I propose the introduction of a relief mark to enrich our expression in the written word. If an exclamation mark is a life mark, I say without a relief mark it is superficial. Relief is life in the positive and negative.

Relief is both a knowing that life is and a knowing that it can so quickly not be. So it is whole in being and not being and there is awareness of both. Hence it is also an expression of gratitude for what is. Exclamation is just stating; relief is wide, embracing being, grateful and knowing. Relief is the giving up when everything has been given; it is acknowledging I am but there is more. This 'more' is what happens when I give all I can, then … It is total. It says, 'Thy will be done not mine.' If an exclamation mark is a life mark, then relief is life regained, a resurrection, life brought back and appreciated, as in, 'Oh, precious life!' Relief is re-life, regaining life, bridging the gap, being blessed again and dissolving the separation between the personality and life. In this sense all life is wonder, but we only appreciate it when we are present or when we experience the threat of no life and then re-gain life.

Relief is to life as the shadow is to the sun. Yes, the sun gives life as visible light, but without shadows it is a one-sided life, without shade and without relief, because when we see something the light gives visibility to the form, and the shadow, the dissolution of the light, emphasises that form. Relief is thus complementary to form in the way that the in and out breath complete each other. Relief is also dissolution: it is when we have stopped holding on, and it is life descending, which makes space for the life ascending. In these modern times, we are so obsessed with doing and making that we forget or ignore the undoing, the ageing, the decaying and the non-being, which are the qualities that make life whole.

So, to get back to being deprived of breath. Breath underlies thought. No breath no thought, or no breath just one thought, 'Life!'

As life is not something we can think about, I would say no thought, just life, or the unthinkable thought, 'God' or whatever your version of the indescribable and always humbling is. We can indulge in thought and be lost in thought, thinking it is life when it is just a pale copy. When breath is taken from us all the stories and ruminations stop, and the only thing that exists is to get breath, so clearly breath comes before thought, otherwise we would just think, 'OK, no breath,' and have that as a thought and ruminate on it, but it is not so. A person who has enquired deeply and persistently as to their true nature may, if deprived of breath to the point of crisis, experience a new life in themselves once breath is re-established, the alive spontaneous current of life. They will feel reborn. This approach is not for the weak of heart or mind. The original baptisms were such, when a person was immersed totally in water, deprived of breath until the crisis point, at which they emerged realising the blessing, the gift that life is, not as a momentary relief but that this gift of life is who we are. That gift, and all we do that has that gift as a foundation, is all we really have to give.

There Is No Noun

Am is meant to represent being, the state that I is in, to be. It is one of those doing words called verbs which are meant to represent actions, but from here AM feels like a noun; it lacks the ing, the zing, the fluidity, the flowing. Aming, yes aming would be better.

Take sitting: when we sit we are actually in a constant state of balancing. If we are watching the body, we will become aware of subtle movements that maintain an approximation of the posture we are holding in our mind. There is nothing called 'I sit'; there is only sitting, a constant adjustment to maintain a posture that never comes to be because *we* are Being. Nothing could become something from Being.

Everything changes with this understanding. Here there is no speech or I speak. 'I' placed before any acting does the damage or it starts the damage. I do not sit and I do not speak. Look at the deadness, the immobility in the statements 'I sit' or 'I speak'. Both I and the action become dead, fixed. There is no speak, there is speaking and there is no I, there is i-ing, also known as living. This becomes evident if we look closely inside and are watching. To watch is to stay separate, but watching involves us, it brings us to life with that which is. Then there is in-derstanding, also known as Understanding. Again, understanding is flowing and we can never say from an inner position that we understand anything. To say we understand anything is again to fix what is flowing and make it into a thing. For I to understand, we also need to fix ourselves, which means we are in the past. We have fixed ourselves in the past and now as a fixed thing we understand through fixing other flowing expressions. Hence the idea 'I understand', but there is no alive understanding as neither what we have fixed nor I is alive here now. Absurd what we do.

Take the statement, 'I speak': it would be better as a first step out of this habit of fixing or freezing things to take the 'I' out of the equation and just leave 'speak'. Now 'speak' sounds more like a command, a willing. If you say to yourself 'speak' rather than 'I speak' you tap into an unknown, you are calling into the void.

Now speak, walk, see and sit and you will notice a shift, because now the underlying force, the inner force, is waking up. We are connecting to that which is deeper than us, that which is hidden inside us, and it starts speaking, walking, seeing and sitting because the I that was covering and even masquerading as being this deeper life force is gone.

We Can Do Nothing but Shine

In modern cities there are streetlights at night and the visibility of the stars is reduced, or they are not seen at all. To see the light of the stars, the natural setting of darkness is needed. The same is true for the light that each person is. That light also requires a natural setting for it to be seen. If we go on gathering knowledge and reflected light, which are second-hand, from objects and thoughts, identifying with all manner of things in an effort to define who we are, then we are obscuring the light that we are with an artificial light. We may feel knowledgeable and protected, but unknowingly we are actually protecting ourselves from the vastness of existence that is our source and also from the light that we are.

The light of each star that stands alone reaches us through the vastness of space. If we are afraid to stand alone, we cannot shine. If we use knowledge or any experience to buttress ourselves, to protect ourselves, then our natural light of being never shines because we are not present. We have denied that we are, denied our true nature and hence only shine as that which we have gathered, appearing as a reflection. This light burns out, this reflection fades. In our attitude of needing knowledge to be who we are, we feel empty. Whereas in reality we are full and overflowing and have all the resources we need to respond to life. We can receive and give, remaining full and present. When we are not at source we are always borrowing and our stores are limited. For the inward journey all knowledge will progressively need to be dropped. When all artificial aids are dropped we can do nothing but shine, because shining is our nature, and we are transmitters of love and light.

What Do We Choose to Stand In?

In moments of insecurity and uncertainty, what we choose as our refuge or support is telling. We can remain present, observe and allow ourselves to feel what is happening, or we can choose to not be present, distract ourselves or filter what is happening through imaginings. If we choose the former course of remaining present with what is, then we stand in the Real. If we choose the latter course of distraction or imaginings, we prolong not seeing our own strength and the strength of existence that always supports when we stand in it, soften and allow.

Each Moment Is a Birth

Each moment is a birth. Each moment is a death opening into rebirth, but if we try to control it there is no opening into birth, only grasping and suffocation in life. Not that life suffocates, but our holding on to life brings about imbalance. Like holding our breath because breath is needed for the body, and then dying through being poisoned by the waste gases we should have expelled. Or understanding that food gives energy and eating ourselves to death – does that sound familiar? Too much life and no death. Too much get and no give. Too much go and no letting. Too much doing smothering being. Our trying to control limits the moment of living, excluding dying, and, although the attempt is to hold life, paradoxically all we are left with is death and dying.

We Have Time or Time Has Us

We either have time or time has us
When we have no time, time has us completely
Having time we forget time

There Is Space

The idea that we do not have time and are overwhelmed with tasks and hence feel we have no space is a mistake, a misinterpretation of what is.

Simply by closing our eyes or directing our attention within, we can feel the space, the limitless inner space that is within us, that inner which we are. This is more real than the things we feel limit and overwhelm us because they appear in that space. This space is omnipresent and the I is a limitation. Even though we fight for this I and cling to it, it is just another of those things that limits and overwhelms us, or you could say we have dressed ourselves up and the costume of our choice is smothering us like a crawling slimy skin in an old sci-fi movie.

Our Job

Existence, or God, makes the differences, the multiplicity. It is not our role to make differences, as we are part of the multiplicity already. Our job is to see the One.

Allowing Thoughts

If a thought is just allowed to be, it goes on its way, but if that thought is resisted for any reason then it goes on to another level where we are not aware of its continuing to function, like a spark we brush under a carpet, and on this other level it works as if it is alive. Yes, each thought is life, and if in sitting meditation we can just allow it to be and actually meet the thought and give it that space, then we are as awareness. Then the thought goes through its life process in that space of awareness and returns to being what it is and where it came from. In this way, thoughts arising in sitting meditation strengthen and deepen understanding of our true nature. Like anything in life, if we can include it, it either becomes an ally or disappears. So it is good to slow down and give ourselves time rather than be in a hurry to achieve something in sitting. In the time we give ourselves, we give space.

We are life and everything we experience is life, and if we refuse to experience it then we have called it death, and it goes on working underground exactly as we have named it until we as life acknowledge it, experience it and feel it. In doing so, we see that we are the source of life beyond any concept we have about life.

When we live life totally, we don't think about it and we don't name it as we *are* it. In seeing this, we can understand that life is not a concept and we don't need a concept to live. When we live totally, we can also see that this experience we named death that we eventually acknowledged and felt cannot harm us, and in understanding both concepts experientially we can move beyond both life and death and the need to live from concepts at all.

Another insight to be gained from just allowing thoughts is that there is no 'in' or 'out', because the line between the individual consciousness (the 'I' thought) and objects (as thoughts) is removed each time a thought is just allowed. Then they are no longer a disturbance, they are just arising and are seen and experienced. The compartmentalising that happens when a thought is resisted and repressed, sent to a level out of sight, is no longer happening. Without compartments there are no lines, just mind being Mind and there is no in or out.

With the absence of lines of separation, the idea of 'me and another' starts to be seen as the self-created construct or illusion that it is, as does the faulty ground of believing in a separate 'me', along with all the ideas of opposites, duality, friendly forces, enemy forces, creative and destructive energies. All are based on an idea of a 'me' and what it wants, which is to survive. Then life gets split into experiences that appear to help or are destructive to this survival. In reality it is all life, which simply requires us to live rather than pro-jecting creativity and destructiveness and then fighting with the reflections. Life is neither for nor against us because we are life, so the decision has been made already.

The Essence of Practice – Stop Trying to Change!

The essence of meditation practice and self-enquiry is to stop try-ing to change **how** we are and experience **that** we are, regardless of what we are feeling or thinking. After all, we know change, so it follows we must be other than change. The trying to change is always being led around by the nose by change. Change is the car-rot: we believe if we can just get hold of it we can stop it, so we put all our effort into going around in circles of trying to change, which is changing to try, because each attempt at change is applied to another new situation or appearance. As we think we have changed, which was our intention, the appearance of what IS changes so we try to change that again, and so the trying and the changing are always shifting. The trying, which starts at the position from which we view the situation, always adopts a new approach, so even the trier is not stable. Hence I say, stop trying to change **how** we are and experience **that** we are, regardless of what we are feeling or thinking.

As we stop trying to change **how** we are and experience **that** we are, there is a shift from doing to being and the true nature of self is revealed.

The Celebration of Our Total Imperfection

Being perfect but striving to be perfect is our inner conflict. We for-get our perfection then strive to be perfect naturally using imperfect means.

The Inner Arising THIS IS IT!

The development of understanding through breath, trust and rest-ing is essential to living and communicating. If we cannot breathe through an experience, we cannot communicate our perception. It is vital that we feel what is, and one way we can do this is through breath. After all, it is spirit that animates matter and this happens in the body through breath.

Breath when used consciously can draw through the whole experience, both in and out of form. Just as when blowing into a wrinkled balloon, the breath reveals the form of the balloon and the more so as the balloon is filled. The person, through breathing consciously, gets to see the forms or form that they are by allowing spirit to enter and inspire them. Through feeling the wounds, tensions and knots of holding and, like the balloon, unwrinkling and becoming who we are, pains that we may have said are holding us back are seen as pains that we are holding on to by imagining we can live fully without experiencing them. In this we can see that it is we who are holding on to the past and in so doing we reinforce the wrinkles and the tensions in our body-mind.

If we could see each breath as an unfolding, an unwrinkling and a moving towards the form of who we are, which when lived through reveals what we are here to do, then what we are here to do is not a command from outside – it is an inner arising, an inner knowing that THIS IS IT!

That Place Beyond Alleviation

I have observed that people often only touch each other or ask to be touched when there is some sickness, pain or tension in the body. Only then it is considered alright to touch and be touched. I have noticed a similarity to this behaviour in the way some people approach their inner journey, or at least the intensity which they bring to it, be it meditation practice or using methods where the tools and the mind are not used to investigate or create but are only used to work out problems. After the problems have been alleviated people's intensity and focus often drop off, but if we persist beyond alleviation and good feelings we will see that the practice also brings forth opening of the heart, beauty, joy in living and celebration, which are the fertile ground for self-realisation. There is an effective use of methods and tools when this purpose is remembered.

Awareness and Consciousness

A person can make a conscious decision. Consciousness is related to I am, as in, 'I am this,' and 'I am not that.' Awareness is aware of consciousness without a 'this' or a 'that'. Awareness is expansive whereas consciousness is specific. Consciousness divides, awareness joins. Awareness requires no prefix, whereas consciousness operates in degrees, which are states of consciousness progressing towards pure consciousness. But ... awareness IS. Awareness is and doesn't come in degrees; hence it does not require the prefix 'pure'. Consciousness is rooted in the idea of objects. The idea of pure consciousness is the idea of consciousness becoming empty of objects, but awareness is aware. It does not require an object, nor does it require to be free of objects.

Working ON

Too much emphasis on solving problems leads to a habit of

working ON
instead of
being
IN

Knowing Intellect's Limitations

Living only through intellect or in our heads, limited to the chatter of the mind, is to live in tension, because when we observe closely we know that the answers intellect gives are not answers; they are just endless commentaries, the opinions and explanations that the intellect contains. These opinions have nothing to do with the actual experience, so we are always left with the Real and the opinions. In this split is our tension, as the commentary that we would like to be the answer, when we limit ourselves to only living through the intellect, is always outside the experience, so it cannot give or be an answer. The answer is in totally experiencing life. The answer is in living and relaxing into life. But before knowing intellect's limitations, it would be cheating ourselves to try to 'think' relaxed or think 'relax'. There is a natural relaxation that comes when everything is in its place, and to 'relax' before this happens is again to let the intellect dictate to us what the natural order is. In doing this we would bypass the challenges and bypass our crystallisation that comes through the tension and pressure, where in spite of not knowing, we persist, being strong enough to be vulnerable and go forward in insecurity, have faith and let go of any idea how we want it to be, but rather be reality.

Who We Are Knows

What arrogance and ignorance to think that we know what is best and that what we do will bring the needed results. We have to realise that the One inside us all, the miracle we are and for which we did nothing, is here. And as that is the case and all has functioned until now thanks to this One, then it makes sense that this One will also do the work, bringing each of us into true functioning once we give ourselves to Her.

So our work is to turn up, be present and remove the obstacles in the way of being here as who we are. That means first being here with no ideas, just being here, and then noticing what is really missing and what really needs changing. And in that space, call it love, peace, detachment or watchfulness, change happens and order happens because the One you are is order, is harmony.

This is not a recipe for the abdication of responsibility and it is not that order or change happens while the individual does nothing. It is so that, through being present, the person now has the potential for change, and they become a vehicle for change because they no longer hinder change through holding ideas. Now, because the individual is turning up without an idea, they can actually see what is. Change, if needed, is then a response to what is. Change is not a compulsion and it is not the imposition of the individual bringing their ideas and memories to the situation. Change is not forced: rather change is literally being present and becoming that which we experience, and responding.

Just look around at how the world fits together, or look closer to home at your body – how it functions without you and your ideas. So, where we remain present as who we are, *there* is the great harmony and order in change, even in loss and death. Remaining is changeless change.

Bin the Carrot – Bring Awareness To

All ideas, words and concepts that purport to represent the possibility of change or correction should be replaced by the idea 'bring awareness to', as there is actually no change or correction. Rather, there is the re-establishment of the true order of consciousness or the reality that comes from awareness. Any concept of change or correction is based on the false idea of a new and better identity. Any correction goes on correcting, correcting and correcting. The corrected version is a copy of the false or abnormal one, which is what cancer is, whereas establishing awareness of what is reveals the obvious, which is always present.

Correction can be seen in social and political programmes where behaviour is corrected without any understanding of the roots of that behaviour, so the correction is just a reaction to what is said to be wrong. This correction may look good in the short term – the situation may appear to be improved – but the investigation has not got to the roots and no real change has actually taken place. Real transformation can only happen at the roots in consciousness, where there is no desire to change but only an unforced, effortless realignment. On seeing what is false, the truth is obvious, and where action is necessary the required action is also obvious. In that the individual is respected and whole, there is no need for outside coercion. The seeing and acting where needed are one whole.

The very act of watchfulness or awareness establishes the truth. Everything else is a distraction.

The Importance of Watchfulness

We need to be watchful of everything so that we don't start to believe that it is real, because what we see are our ideas about the world, and if we are not watchful then these ideas that were once born from us will take on a life of their own. We will start to believe that these ideas are independent actors who act against us, control us or do anything they like to us. It is like when as children we would play games, imagining what was in the darkness in the bedroom or in deserted unlit buildings, until we had charged the space with so much of our imagination that we became scared (of our own imagination). We do it all the time, and it is especially noticeable in actions we regret or actions which are destructive, and it goes a bit like this. We are meandering along living our life and we get a thought, and we think about this thought: 'Hmm, that would be interesting to experience.' And the thought and the interest grow until we start doing the actions dictated by that thought so we can really experience what it is, because we consider it interesting, forgetting our depth and that we are the miracle – the most ultimately endless and interesting one.

We go on doing this, gradually forgetting more and more that WE ARE DOING IT and that it is our imagining creating a picture story. We do this until we fall into the mirror and become the image, having moved from being watchful to being that which we were watching. Then the story really starts being interesting, except there is no one to be interested any more.

We invest attention and get interest. The attention and the interest is all our doing, through focusing and perceiving. After all, interest is interest in oneself. Interest is the reflection of our focused consciousness, which is our attention, from the surface of an object or thought. So we are giving attention to ourselves via an object or thought. This understanding shows us that we are everything and nothing, and it opens up a lot of possibilities concerning being non-judgemental. After all, who would judge themselves? Yes, a mind without an owner – a loose mind – does do that, but when there is the understanding that this perception coming back to us is an echo of ourselves, of our own focused consciousness called attention, then we perceive our world very differently.

The Light of Noticing

We only notice the light directly when we have just flicked the switch. In that moment, we notice there is light, and if not, perhaps the bulb is broken. In the case of no light, we have noticed what is not here because we had an expectation that it would be here. But we are the light of awareness noticing whether our expectations are fulfilled or not. If we can realise this then our light is on.

If a person can become aware of the moment when the switch is flicked and the light comes on or not, or become aware of the moment the impulse arose to flick that switch, and find the source of that impulse, then one becomes centred and awake. Centred like the source emitting light, the light that is on and shines on all the objects in the room but still remains as it is. Light cannot be dirtied or stained – it is always fresh now. That is our quality when we are source.

Then we are noticing and whole, we are as if twice found – not found and then lost in objects but found realised as light *and* seeing the objects. Being through seeing. So finding is being, the finding of that which was never missing or had never been lost, like the electricity in the wires. Whether or not the switch is flicked or the bulb is broken, the electricity IS.

All Directions and Dimensions Are of Me

Whatever I see is in me. If I see it, it is in me. All directions and dimensions are in me and they are of me – I am the centre from which they emerge. Take here and there – they are in me. They are not here or there – they are in me. They are me. I arm them, and they arm me. Then they are me with possibility. Am I not infinite possibility armed in the present with my past and future? That past that has gone in me and the future that is appearing through me constantly. But the future appearing I call the present and it arrives as the present having already been seen. But what a surprise!

'I' sees things, and because 'I' identifies with the body and because the human body is so constructed that our eyes are at the front of our heads, we 'think' we see forwards. This reflects in our language and our outlook, both physically and in any vision we might have. We think we are the body, a thing. and this thing is structured to look forwards and hence this thing we identify with sees things, the extensions of itself as it looks forwards. And it also looks forward to things. But the more we look inside, the more a new looking develops, a non-moving looking, a non-aggressive looking, which is seeing. Because what we are looking at and enquiring into is our original nature, which is always here, so we are not looking forwards, not getting, discovering or creating anything. We call it looking in because our language is extrovert, but actually we do not go anywhere or look anywhere, but rather by becoming what we are, we see, and this seeing is being or this seeing is feeling-being. It is awareness of what is, which is Being. This Being is in all forms – it is not just an individual separate being seeing. No, that is the old aggressive looking – this is now Being-seeing feeling itself in all forms.

As we look 'in', the mind stops. That 'in' is here, and that 'in' arrives at who we are. Call it what you will – all words fail – but the main thing is to start, because this is the only way to go beyond duality and all the hollow promises of words and concepts.

Deepening into Being is also Being being seen. Separation dissolves and movement as direction also dissolves here. See. We see trees but trees see us. It must be this way when Being is in all forms. Now that which is being and seeing in the tree is the same being seeing in us, so in the same way that we can say we see trees or trees see us we can also experience that we are trees and trees are us. What is it that responds in the tree, as scientists have measured trees doing, when it senses that certain presence of a person who wants to cut the tree down? For the word 'senses' we can also say 'feels', because all senses are a form of touch, of feeling. So, what is it in the tree which *feels* that certain presence of a person who wants to cut the tree down?

Seeing/feeling and being, and awareness of being are not separate. There is no seeing something, as in the experience of seeing through body identification, but by looking inside – which is stopping the mind – and being we see that we are. We are THAT which we see as we merge into it. With no separation, Being is seeing, and the process of seeing all as Being and not separate begins, which is the process of becoming love.

Then there is no seeing something, as in the experience of seeing as a body-mind by that somebody that you call yourself: the sum body, the accumulation of all the body of ideas, the body of emotions, the body of sensations, and so on. By looking inside – which is stopping the mind – and being nobody, we merge into no-mind, no-body, no any-thing. Now I am, and I include bodies and no-bodies, things and no-things. Which brings me full circle back to what I wrote at the beginning of the essay: 'Am I not infinite possibility armed in the present with my past and future? That past that has gone in me and the future that is appearing through me constantly.'

So I am that in which everything merges. Nothing ever kills me and I don't die – I merge in what I am. Being. Being we can never deny, and hence it is always, but it is not a thing or nothing, not a somebody or nobody, not mind or no-mind, because all these disappear in it.

Being what we are, we use mind, whose language is concepts, to be in form.

Awareness (Is, formless, without content). Being (forms – seeing/feeling). Being – a form through which awareness manifests and experiences itself through being/feeling/seeing. For the logical mind it appears as two, but for awareness nothing has changed – it is still one. One being, one experiencing.

No-Self Service

Not self help but Self service.
Not self help, no-self service.

Unblinking is – Is is Unblinking

We perceive everything – EVERYTHING. We are Aware of everything, like an unblinking eye. As awareness we are continuous, which is why under hypnosis or in deep relaxation we can remember events that we thought we had forgotten or had no conscious memory of experiencing. We collect memories to define who we are, as opposed to remaining as awareness, and then we create a split into me and the world. In this 'me and the world' we deny certain things as who we are not and affirm others as who we are. But, because we are Awareness, we are aware of both and we are both. Without Self-Awareness, these things which we affirm and deny would not exist, so we must be they and we are inextricably woven together with them. So, if there is any rejection or denial in us, it is only a matter of time until we become that which we are denying, because our whole movement is towards wholeness and we *are* whole. It is just a trick, an illusion which we actively create. So let's call it self-delusion, because we do it to ourselves, imagining, 'I am this. I am not that.' If we see something, it must be in us. For anything to be in us, we the awareness must be here first, which means awareness also comes before who we think we are, because who we think we are is a result of the process of denials and affirmations.

Nobody the Know-Body

We are so in the habit of doing that when we sit in meditation we can sometimes turn this also into a doing. We can think that still, even here, we have so much to work out and work on, but sitting is not the place for this. In the world, we work things out and work on things. Sometimes it seems to me that the 'inner world' and the 'outer world' have completely different movements, as if one is the inverted form and function of the other. For instance, to know in the outer world is to know some-thing and be some-body, but to know in the inner world is to know no-thing – it is to be. To be no-body is the know-body. The know-body being the who-we-are, our true nature, which just knows, without any knowledge or objects to support its knowing. So it is the no-know-body. It is knowing without, and hence it is within.

The habit of working out suggests an in and an out, but show me an out which is not in. The habit of working on suggests somebody being outside the thing they intend to work on. So when we sit and try to work on things, we are still attempting to know and understand things or see them clearly, but by using this approach we can only know things in time. This knowing is bringing in memory and comparison, which are time-based, whereas the inner knowing radically cuts through any time, because the knower is here, out of time. The knower or seer sees but is never seen. So when Jesus the Christ says, 'Be still and know that I am God,' he means be out of time, be not objectifying, no working out or working on. Just, 'Know I am.'

All knowledge is good, all working out and working on, and all techniques and methods are good, but ultimately, presently, that which has never needed work or time will be revealed. It cannot be any other way, because it came before all the objects, ideas and desires and all these are expressions of it. 'Be still and know that I am God.' All doing is leading to and arises from that which we ultimately realise as who we are, and we can ask where it all comes from and return to our centre or we can watch it all, see it settle and in that settling return to the source, our centre, the place where all of it comes to rest and from whence it arose.

The knower is still here. The knower is still here!

The Neighbourhood of the Mind

A short reflection on mind and the importance of getting to know it and hence our self, so we do not live in a state of reaction to it, but through knowing it we can befriend it and use it as the tool that it is.

We have to get to know the neighbourhood of our mind and get involved in it. Then we will know how to penetrate it, how to move in it and how to manifest the potential of it. The more we move in it, the more we learn how it fits together. Then it is no longer a puzzle for us, and whichever piece we are confronted with we know exactly where we are and where the piece fits together with the other pieces. Then the neighbourhood is always whole, as it is familiar from wherever we approach it.

Our Best Friends Could Be Actors (if we'd let them)

It is interesting to see that we enjoy and appreciate a person called an actor playing different roles while still accepting that they are the same person, but may struggle to allow a person close to us the same freedom. We believe in the fixedness of the person whom we think we know, but really it is only our thinking which is fixed, and it is that which we project on the person. Maybe we would enjoy ourselves more and appreciate the people in our lives if we allowed them to play different roles.

For Healing

For healing, we need to move to a place where all we have learnt is forgotten, and then in expressing from this original place all is remembered, that is, everything as a part finds its place.

Moving in Mind

It is evident that I am not my mind when I move in it. When living in a house, the house serves a function, but it does not dictate which rooms the owner can move in or what the owner can do in those rooms.

To follow a thought back to its source is to move in mind. This ability to move involves letting go of where we think we are and who we think we are. It is stepping out of the film that is running. In stopping and seeing the gap, the non-solidity of the mind, we discover mind's non-existence.

This is soft and light falling.

Thought Is Not at Fault

It is not thought that is at fault, so do not try to get rid of thoughts – that you can never do. Thought has its place and exists as everything else does. We are the problem when we identify with thought, so being ourselves and letting thought be itself is liberating.

*

It is the I thought that gives power to all the other concepts in mind. Without a person identifying with the concept 'I' in the statement, 'I am right', that concept carries less weight. The concept 'right' alone is a neutral concept when not identified with. The power and meaning come when it is combined with a person's mind with the root thought I, or in other words a persona called I. Say to yourself 'right' or 'I am right' and feel the difference. The only difference is 'I am'. But both the 'I' and the 'am' as concepts are lifeless, so what brings life? Clearly it must be the non-conceptual sense of being, that which comes before concept and thought, because in the same way that 'right' comes alive when combined with the 'I' and 'am' concepts, 'I am' comes alive when that which is before concepts brings itself to the concept 'I am'. So who is the non-conceptual that brings life to all concepts? Who IS without concepts and who or what do all concepts require for them to manifest? Who is this before concept arises and who remains after concepts, including the I concept, disappear? Clearly you. Of course, concept-free.

Centres

As the centre is still, everything which emanates or arises from the centre must also be still, even as it appears to move or change.

The centre is still
Stillness is alive
It is born and dies
Comes and goes
So alive is stillness
The centre.

The centre is not: it is only a concept, a reference point for all peripheries and circumferences. The centre is the place where all peripheries and circumferences arise and where they all return to. It is from the centre that all form and space arise and it is where they return to, but we never find that centre. How could we, because a 'we' is a form as is an 'I', and for I to find the place I arise from would be my demise. Hence, in consciousness, I am always separate from my centre, otherwise I am not. As Awareness there is no objectifying that which I am and that means no object called a centre.

Form Returns to Centre

Form returns to the centre when it is of essence. Form carries the essential qualities of its centre from whence it came, namely emptiness, stillness and potential. The very act of returning is renunciation, is sacrifice and it is as Jesus said, that the rich man would be unable to get through the eye of the needle even if the camel could pass through.

The one who is willing to let go can return. Jesus the Christ also expressed this in, 'Blessed are the poor for they shall inherit the kingdom of heaven,' with 'poor' meaning not having accumulated and held on to form. Where form is not held and there is no attachment to that which has arisen from the still centre, then that which returns is as pure as that which arose. Hence it can return in its totality, as there is no difference between essence and form, no difference between the periphery and the centre, and no difference between the in breath and the out breath.

In the breathing cycle, attachment and accumulation would be like always withholding a part of the air inhaled as a percentage tax, and this part, a progressively growing volume, would eventually kill us. Life held is life killed: it is a collectively accepted and respected form of suicide. That breath which nourished when fresh becomes death when not released.

Or consider the case of a punctured lung, where the air is leaking out and we never get a full breath. If we shy away from life and don't face it directly, we never fully receive life. Perhaps we feel over-whelmed and unable to contain our experiences of living. Then life received is not seen as a fulfilment and is constantly leaked or fil-tered. A natural breathing rhythm can never take place, and exhala-tion is experienced as an act of defeat and not the fulfilment of inspiration.

*

Too much life poisons us to death. Too little and we die, withering away from lack. Do we see this around us or not?

*

Real forms preserve life, embrace and sustain all beings. As they know they owe their existence to stillness, emptiness and potential they maintain, sustain and embrace stillness, emptiness and potential.

*

An old-style vinyl record has, when it sits rotating on the turntable, a still centre as does a real person. When one groove or one – ANY! – personality characteristic takes over in a person then the founda-tion is no longer real as the form does not return to the centre, its foundation. Then there is repetition of form as opposed to repetition through emptiness. A part of the music is too dominant, or the guitar-ist wants to hog the stage and be the centre of attention. This centre is then full of form, full and too visible. The real centre is invisible. It is just what it is, the centre. It does not need to appear or announce itself – it is affirmed by the existence of all that surrounds it.

X does not mark the spot.

The art of form or the true form of art is to create form which is empty, still and potential. A form which inspires, that is which breathes these qualities into the observer, or enables the observer to become aware of these qualities they already have within. This art creates a space where the observer can be empty, free of form, thought and ideas. For this, the artist will need to have glimpsed, touched or know these qualities. The best practitioner knows, and through what is created the observer remembers. Re-members, meaning the observer crystallises, and all these qualities that were previously scattered, all forms that as fragments made up the observer, come together so there is a real form, a member, cohesive sensing and hence a real centre. The real form and the real centre appear together, and this centre is still, empty and has the potential to manifest.

*

The real form is whole: it is not aware of itself other than being aware. It is and it is not. It is full and empty. It has a centre, a root, and it is its own centre. It is indestructible for all these reasons. Like a wave is a wave, but it is also the ocean. The ocean is its home, its centre, its ground, but it also exists as a wave. This wave is a centre unto itself and the ocean is its centre, and there is no conflict here.

If It's Tight in There

It will always be tight unless we are moving or have moved beyond our small self and ideas. The Twelve Step community have the right idea here in relying on a power greater than themselves. So we are all addicts ultimately addicted to who we think we are. Addicted to our thoughts and beliefs we call our own, and which we make into that me, that small self. Addicted ultimately to 'I' and not allowing the grace of life, that greater existence which is who we are and is greater than who we are, to be the mover in us.

Balance

Balance is in all parts of the body: it is everywhere and nowhere. When I want to stand on a balance board* I start by pressing down on one foot,

---

* A balance board is a board used by surfers to train on. It consists of a roll of hard plastic on which a wooden board is placed. The surfer then stands with feet apart on the board, balancing on the plastic roll, so that both feet are off the ground. It's great body training, fun and revealing.

and this one foot dominates in the service of balance. When the other foot comes into play, that one dominates for a time while the other foot surrenders and relaxes, until balance is established and neither foot dominates. Balance is in both feet and nowhere. No one foot rules and no one foot balances. Here, I saw that balance is alive. The feet die to balance and they serve balance. Balance is somewhere, though nobody can say where, but still balance is, and it is alive stillness.

We are in an imbalanced balance, an evolving out-of-control harmony.

In life, contradictions can exist and together make a whole, but then we need to be non-localised in the same way that balance is non-localised. The fact that there are contradictions introduces imbalance.

If there was nothing, then there would be absolute balance. But as the elements, whatever they are, originally come from – or 'come out of' – nothing, then balance is inherent in them. It is funny to write and read 'come out of balance', which also means that what has appeared comes out of or from balance, making it clear that balance is the sub-stratum. Only when we don't see the substratum or be the substratum do things then look out of balance. As soon as anything appears there is imbalance, but intuitively it must also equate that if something has appeared to bring about imbalance a some-thing has also appeared which complements it and which maintains the balance. So existence, the mystery, the higher order, is also a landlord (in the good sense) as it keeps order. Yes, the land Lord maintains order regardless of who moves into the house, because he knows how it should be. The deeper we go and the more elements as contradictions, or imbalances, we experience the more existential we become: we literally become exis-tence and balance as we go, see and feel. So it is up to the individual to be ALL, maintain balance and be watchful and aware, which is the Buddha's middle way. Otherwise we suffer because we see imbal-ance and try, from our separate position, to maintain balance, but this cannot be done until we include the complementary or opposite.

'Inside' Is One

When we close our eyes. But not limited to when we close our eyes.

If we close our eyes and are aware of what we experience, we will realise that there is no inside or outside. This is the realisation of the Oneness of All. It all happens inside or outside and this appearing to happen depends on where you decide to locate yourself. But really there are no lines or boundaries. There is just awareness.

Anything which we experience Is. It is neither here nor there, up nor down, in nor out: it just Is (and it is who we are). To remain 'in' is to let go of the ideas of in and out and present, future and past. It is one whole and indivisible. It is That which everybody is and it is That which everybody strives for.

Anything we can get is separate from us. We say we got it, and we know as we say this that we can lose it, and so we experience fear. The getting says it is not a part of me, it is outside of me, now I have brought it into me, but that me is separate and the desire fulfilled is also separate. Once it was outside and now it is inside. The real happiness is inside, the inside which has no outside, which language cannot express but everybody knows when they stop going out, when they go in.

If we close our eyes and remain aware of what we experience, we will realise that there is no inside or outside.

The Natural State Is Natural

To not be in the natural state is as impossible as not having your feet on the ground as a result of gravity. Under gravity, resting on the earth, our bodies don't fly around. Resting in the natural state, our mind doesn't fly around.

Stateless

If we were dropped anywhere on the planet with no idea where we were, we would be somewhere but unable to put a label on it. Labels would appear and ideas grow as we came into contact with the signs of nature and the structures and signs that humans had left behind. These signs would trigger the inner signs in our memory. Seeing these signs on the outside would give us an idea of what part of the world or country we were in.

If we have no external input through such signs, after a while we move into another way of being, more flexible and more connected to the environment and nature. So, even though our memories contain signs, concepts and language, without an outer response or mirroring these subside, being of no present use, and then other signs such as climate, sounds, smell and terrain take priority.

Inner peace is as stateless as being dropped into somewhere devoid of signs and labels referring to its location. Inner peace has no signs: it is deeper than the mind of signs and memory. It is the mind but without content.

A car in neutral with the engine started is full of potential.

Stateless – A Method

Surrender to all states and be as if dropped into an area of wilderness devoid of signs or dropped into space. Relate from this stateless state. Be stateless. In the event of any states or signs arising, the instructions are 'Let go.'

Being Is Re-Maining

If we fall into a stormy ocean, even though the ocean is rough and we are thrown about and pulled under by the waves, we still know where we need to go to survive. We still know it is the air that will sustain us and we know where to go to get air. In fact we are pushed up: we naturally float upwards in the water.

As in the waves of the ocean, so it is in the inner journey. In challenging situations, in crises, we know who we are and act accordingly, despite the confusion and pain. When we stop fighting life we rise, we see the way out, or we are lifted out of the turbulence. The more we stop in life, the more we see we are awareness, which knows the way. In the same way that we move upwards for air in the ocean, in life we move towards our natural state of being, which is our sustenance regardless of what is happening.

Life appears turbulent until we stop and remain as and what we are. It is our re-action to the situations in life which makes it seem turbulent, like the drowning man who does himself no service by splashing around more when someone comes close to save him, or in a misunderstanding when the heat of emotion makes communication less effective, where stopping and listening would serve us better. Turbulent is our chosen way to look at life. Instead, we could see it as alive, a miracle, and we could be passionate about it, engrossed in it, fascinated by it, inquisitive and curious about it, it being who and what we are.

Life is who we are in the manifest, as appearance. The life we experience is the product of our actions, and our feeling buffeted by life is our re-action, or the action resulting from a previous action, and in this we become an echo not the source. What we have done is separated our selves off, and through this we experience 'life' and 'me' as distinct.

The required journey is one of stepping back into life and remaining aware. Remaining aware means re-maining, plugging into the main stream, the life force. This re-maining is the antidote to separating off and re-acting. It requires that we feel and be. Re-maining is active: it requires effort, like balancing until there is stability. This balance is dynamic. It is the conclusion of opposites where we again become centred. And it is this dynamism which is alive, because in the experience of centredness the point is not to hold beingness as fixed: this would again be separating from the main current, which always flows.

To let go of being is to let go of the idea of how being should be and live as awareness in the world. It is the peak of Zen expressed through the Tenth Bull of Zen, which Osho spoke about in his book *The Search*. When we enter life, we enter the whole and become whole. For the mind this whole is made up of opposites, whereas in awareness life is whole as awareness includes all: awareness joins.

To be, or not to be, is still the question.
This ache for being is the ultimate hunger.
And for myself, I can say 'almost, almost, oh, very nearly.'
Yet something remains.
Something shall not always remain.
For the main already is fulfilment.

D. H. Lawrence – *Manifesto* (verse VI), from *The Complete Poems of D. H. Lawrence*.

To Go In Is to Be Here

To go in is to be here
To be here is to have no hold

To have no hold is to let go
To let go is to be unburdened
And to be unburdened is to be light.

Normally, we bring in or cling on to thoughts and feelings to support ourselves and keep up our self-image, to avoid feeling what is. We construct any thing to not feel the emptiness. Here is here and as we go in and feel here, first as form and then progressively deeper, we come to feeling, pure feeling, being here. And this being here is indivisible. Being and here are just different ways of expressing the same thing, as here is the only place to be and being can only be here. It is good to understand this, as it opens up two paths to the realisation of having no hold, starting either from 'being' or from 'here'.

In is in: it has no direction. Usually when we think in terms of things, we think of going somewhere or getting something, so going in is strange because in is: in is the root of all goings and gettings. As in has no direction or content, the person who is used to clinging to an object is at a loss or feels lost, having no thing to hold on to and hence no idea of who they are. But the blessing in this is that any knowing just clouds being, so to feel this loss, this sense of not having anything to hold on to, is good. Now, having no idea reveals the space for the real. Where previously ideas clouded the real, now the 'I', admitting its downfall and humbled at having no idea, can be what it is, consciousness free of ideas, free of content. Because here we realise and here we see. As Thomas Merton writes in *Zen and the Birds of Appetite*:

> Zen enriches no one. There is no body to be found. The birds may come and circle for a while in the place where it is thought to be but they soon go elsewhere. When they are gone, the 'nothing', the 'nobody' that was there, suddenly appears. That is Zen. It was there all the time but scavengers missed it, because it was not their kind of prey.

It was not their kind of prey because they preferred the dead over the living, or they preferred death over life. Better they had circled and encircled and penetrated themselves, been prey to themselves. Looked in and not out and while looking in pecked deep, that is used their desire to find the content desired and the source of that desire.

Ideas collect more ideas, but none are satisfying because they all miss the reality. When we remain with having no idea, only that can bring contentment, because that ground is open: it is in harmony with our original nature.

Oh, what beauty
What freedom
Just to know this
To hear these words
And know this possibility exists
And is with each person
In Here

At a loss?
Lose yourself
Go in, going, gone

Broken Hearts

In sitting and observing the pressure of the physical heart or chest and the release beyond it when we lay down that which we have been carrying, having thought we were the doers, then there is Heart, or that which makes all this possible and meaningful. There we can allow life to carry life, ourselves included.

A heavy or broken heart is a great opening for transcending and hence integrating all we carry. And all we carry is what we think we are, so the breaking of that which we think we are – in other words the false – the breaking of that heart, is an awakening to who we are. The false broken reveals the true whole; hence the physical body and the heart are gateways to the spirit. The physical heart is a gateway to the spiritual heart. It is we who hold things and thus make them physical. The spiritual heart requires no holding because it IS, so it cannot be attacked or broken.

Hearts need to be broken, otherwise how can God, life, existence enter and flow through us?

Daisies from Blossoming Hearts

Non-action and silent awareness are present in every action; they arise and shine when we have given up.

Every mourner's wish and priest's funeral speech goes on about resting in peace. Why wait? Practise now! Push up and push out the daisies from your blossoming heart.

Rest in peace, rest in peace
May he or she rest in peace
May we live in peace without a may
The heart's desire, our inner command
Live in peace vitally.

Aloneness

Once I was at an airport and it was evening and dark. I was there to pick somebody up, but they were delayed for a long time. I had time to myself and I just felt loneliness. I didn't do anything to get rid of it. I breathed into it and went for a walk, just feeling alone. I didn't phone anybody. I just walked, and after a while the discomfort became less, the impulse to do something, to connect, to do anything but feel exactly this loneliness dropped away, and I was just alone in a large concrete multi-storey car park in an airport and it was okay.

This has stayed with me and in many situations it sheds light on what is happening. For instance, I became more aware of how much I felt like an outsider, and without changing anything I became that outsider who, strangely, is not an outsider or an insider but rather a response to the situation. Because, as I started to enjoy being an outsider, I could relax into and fill out that costume and from there relate, respond, share, speak and act, or not, because the driving force was no longer to merge with another or withdraw from the other but rather to be. It seems as though only the outsider is truly free. Everybody else is bound by wanting to belong or suffering being apart or variations on this theme, such as suffering belonging and at the same time wanting to be separate but not having the courage. Or wanting to belong, but being in so much pain that the person cannot come out of their outsider shell or through their outsider armour.

So truly being an outsider can be liberating from the push and pull of belonging and withdrawing. Now from here I experienced, through loneliness leading to aloneness, how small I am. As soon as I felt this, I also felt how big I am, how vulnerable I am and in the same moment how indestructible I am. I saw that avoiding loneliness through belonging is a social way for a person to believe they can make themselves immortal or indestructible: being a member of a club, having their name on a brass commemoration plaque, being recognised and remembered. But nobody is immortal. Those who are compelled to belong to a system because they believe they are lacking are dependent on and at the mercy of that system, which can pull the plug on them at any moment. That seems to be why social systems that proclaim to provide for the well-being of their members always seem to fail, because yes there could be enough for all – as we know there is enough food to feed everyone on the planet – but the very drive that motivates a person to be part of the system is based on fear, especially the fear of death and not having enough and being vulnerable. So although the system is designed to provide for all and all profess to be in and support the vision of the system, most act to take more and accumulate more than they need for living, and then everybody sees this happening around them and that in turn amplifies the fear that there will not be enough, so people need more and it goes on and on.

I believe that a social system will only work when it has a spiritual base to it, a base that acknowledges both our identity as the body and the needs thereof and our truth as spirit, a system designed to promote insight into our true nature. Then resources can be channelled into those goals that support basic needs, but those basic needs are in turn a support for the enquiry into our true nature.

So the walk went on in this fashion and this fashion has, as you can read, continued to shed light on my life and life as I observe it. Feeling, knowing I am tiny, tiny, tiny and totally dependent, where the mystery can pull the plug on me at any moment, but this means I am plugged into God and co. (a.k.a. existence) right now.

Existence is pouring into me right now whether I am separate or connected to others, and that brought me to another complementary insight. I am totally separate. The whole idea of feeling myself to be an outsider was itself a protection, a denial of what is, a costume smothering and covering who I am. I am totally separate: nothing of who I am is related in any way to anything else. That I am is not a product or effect of any cause. It is this idea of cause and effect that drives a person unconsciously to want to belong. They think in the right environment they will experience the right cause to make them be who they are, but that is stating that a person is an effect. Yes a person, a personality, a mask may be an effect but a being is not, nor is our true nature.

I felt separate and it was okay, and in this separateness I felt connected, porous and transparent. By being separate I became. By being separate I became connected. I finally and again appeared through an illusion. I became dependent on the source of all being, which I am, which is in me and all around me.

Oceanic

We are waves often trying to take comfort in being forms in the ocean, but this comfort is always short-lived. The comfort becomes discomfort, as we have been clinging to the form and feel forced to let go when the wave breaks. The blessing in this is that every time we break, we become oceanic. This breaking can take any form; it is basically the movement from what we desire and feel we have and are, to something we do not know and do not want.

The breaking is the transition; it is the place of not knowing, which is with us all the time if we are observant. The mind desiring to be knowing thinks it has solidity and it would like to jump from one knowing to another knowing, but in this we miss the vastness that is actually flowing through and surrounding these small islands of knowing. The vastness is not-knowing, though not as the opposite to knowing, but as the stuff which makes knowing and the conventional not knowing possible.

The breaking is a reminder that it is time to move on and that where we had stayed overnight is not our home, a reminder that everything is transient. A loved one dies or an animal friend dies. Or we imagine we have achieved some sweet blissful untouchable space in our meditation and we try to fix it in place. Then here, also, we will have to experience the breaking, as the sweet will become sour sooner or later.

Vertical Breath

Breath and mind when under the influence of the ego, which fears constantly for its existence, operate horizontally – always going somewhere trying to get something. When we watch the breath and allow whatever is, without holding on to it, then the breath leads us in and we arrive here. Breath observed is experienced as it is, a cycle, and we drop in on breath, entering the verticality of the moment. We never arrive where the egoic mind tries to lead us with its ever extending horizontal promises. We are always here, and we can watch the breath and follow the breath. With the mind thus tethered, we are out of the horizontal and in the vertical present.

Poles – I Am Not Feeling Myself

The 'I', having two ends, has polarities: plus–minus, win–lose, me–you, etc., when laid horizontally. When seen or rather experienced vertically, that is now, the two poles are That and I. Even the form negates distance and is the figure, the number one. The more a person holds the thought, 'That Am I,' the more the mind with all its polarities merges into That. We cannot deny I or That as they are the base elements of Being. I cannot deny Being and at the same time intuit that I have a source, that there is something greater than I.

Now let us take 'me'. Me is already a pollution of I as I does not possess anything. Me is already an echo, a copy of I. Although me thinks it possesses, as in 'mine', the opposite is the truth: me is possessed. It is like looking in a reflection: everything is not where it appears to be. We know that the eye turns the image around and that we re-turn the image, but now there is so much false money in circulation that nobody remembers anymore what the original currency looks like. Me owes its existence to the Real and always returns to That. In the delusion of me, me is possessed by ideas. Like the drunk who thinks he can do it better with a few drinks, the alcohol starts to speak not the drinker, still …

I am. I am not me. Funny when people say, 'I am not feeling myself,' as if their self were something like feeling hot or cold or something they possessed, when really they themselves possess this 'myself' idea, and all that is happening is that what they are experiencing does not fit with that idea or those ideas which they hold themselves to be. Tip: find the experiencer.

There Is More to I than Me

We all know there is more to I than me and unless all is mine I am not. I am and all is mine because that is what I call me; then for all to be mine I would need to be bigger than all. Then who am I if nothing defines who I am, as I am bigger than and contain all? So this 'me' we could say is what is possessed by the thought 'I', which means that if 'me' is how we define ourselves we are our own jailers and create our own suffering. So the Buddha was right: life is suffering, the life for a 'me'.

On Losing Balance

When we lose our balance physically the solution is not to regain balance. Balance seen in this way is the outer idea of being stable. Trying to balance like this results in swinging from one extreme to the other, whereas what we need to do is bend the knees, sink down and come closer to the earth, lower our centre of gravity and stop trying to reach the Gods and be above everything. We need to come down and befriend the lower. Or, when experiencing imbalance in the mind, we need to sink in and come closer to that which disturbs us. Maybe that is what understand means: to understand we stand under, we go down and know the underlying.

As Laotse says in the poem, Water:

> The best of men is like water;
> Water benefits all things
> And does not compete with them.
> It dwells in (the lowly) places that all disdain –
> Wherein it comes near to the Tao.

From *The Wisdom of Laotse* by Lin Yutang

Harnessing the Life Force

A man driving a horse-drawn carriage puts the harness around the shoulders and the torso of the horse, as this is where the life force is. Where do *we* harness the life force in our bodies when we want to move and do? The head or the heart won't do, as they have no gravity to transfer movement. To move effectively, we must sit in the saddle of the pelvis and be centred in our bellies at the root of our life force, in what the Japanese call the hara. We need to breathe down and direct our attention into the root of our life force. In that ground we balance, we anchor and purify the drifting mind, bringing it back to its root. From the branches and the leaves that fall off in the autumn, we bring it back down to where everything arose from.

Slipping

Babies don't know how walking works. They fall, but they want to stand up and walk, as this is the world they see around them and they wish to be a part of it. When we live and practise, we slip, fall, make mistakes and get distracted, but we are aware and also know the destination, it being who we really are. All this slipping, falling and getting distracted is a good sign and always the place to start.

Walking

Walking with the body involves the sensations and at times the pains of our body. When we are simply aware of walking, those sensations are the experience of walking. They *are* walking in the same way that our life *is* life – it is all we are experiencing.

If we are living, meeting and enjoying our life, our dreams and what life brings to us, we are integrating life as we go and our life is whole. The trials of life also belong to life that is life.

In being with the sensations and pains of walking, there is also the question, how far are you from here or, how far are you from being everything? In sitting meditation there is the same question, until there is no question. Or sitting opposite another person, how far are you from being everything, which here now includes the other as experienced in yourself? Life ongoing is life going on.

Our Obsession with Knowing – Nourish the Gap

We have an obsession with knowing everything, with seeing every thing, and it doesn't bring us anything. Consider that most communications through the media – and also social exchanges – are made palatable to us, so they fit and we will swallow them. These communications fit the image we carry of our self, the 'I' idea which is our personality. They don't challenge what we believe and they don't provoke change, doubt or questioning. When the communication fits to our idea we immediately feel in control, so nothing has changed. There was a brief healthy moment of receptivity, a gap, a not knowing. But once we have accepted another image, that of the speaker together with the idea, we continue as before, having consumed the new. Remember it was made palatable for us. Then the idea is older and deader than before, like we ourselves are as we become filled with ideas and through that bigger, heavier, denser, more protective. Heavy. A dead weight.

When we miss the gap, we miss the gold that is the moment of not knowing. I mean, what is the point of knowing if it is not knowing now? What is this knowing then but a dream, something which is not here, and although you may dream when you live in London that you are in New York, when you wake up you don't plan a day trip to the Empire State Building. No, when we wake up our sense experience is now, and that is what we desire and need, to see reality. What use is knowing about something that went before in the journey of self-discovery? Knowing what went before is of help in science, in programming computers or robots and in any study where there seem to be fixed laws. But in yourself, where you are not bound by laws, now where this moment's perception is, what use does the past have? Because even to perceive what is now in the application of what we 'think' has gone before, we would need a 'not knowing place', otherwise the present time perception would be coloured and distorted by our thought. For 'thought' read memory, our past perception.

Hammer on the rock of this obsession. This is the work, if we desire to extricate ourselves from the net of palatable communications and the dead weight of our self-image. On the London Underground, they have an announcement at some stations which says, 'Mind the gap.' That is what we do when we are obsessed with knowing: we throw our mind into the gap and that mind is full of ideas, so there is no space for what is now. The subtitle of this piece is Nourish The Gap, because only in the gap of 'now' can we really perceive; anything else is remembering or anticipating. Still, on a physical level we do need to 'Mind the doors.'

Stepping Off the Rock

In watchfulness there is still the subject being an object. To let go of this object we have made of our self is to let go into the space of being. The object we make our self into is conditioned consciousness, whereas awareness is unconditioned. As object we are surrounded by oceanic space. Letting go is stepping off the rock into that space.

Desiring to Know or Be the Knower

Desiring to know or be the knower is like deciding what we want to see, writing all of it down on paper, cutting up the paper with a word on each piece and then sticking the pieces onto our glasses, with the words facing towards us. Or in Zen language it is covering your mirror with the pieces of paper, still hoping the mirror will reflect. A woman knows that sticking a picture of the current idea of beauty in women over her mirror does not make her beautiful when she looks into that mirror. Now, of course, in all these cases the mirror cannot reflect, the glasses are not transparent and consciousness is covered. We see, but what we see is all our preconceived ideas written on the paper pieces that cover the mirror or our glasses or are stuck in our consciousness. All we see is all we thought, and wanted to see, before we looked. We are not sensitive and transparent; we cannot reflect anew in the moment. Seeing or wisdom is not possible, because what we then know is what we always knew, and what we see is what we have decided to see.

No Wonder

When we don't look
It is no wonder
We can't see

When we can't be
It is no wonder
That we can't do

When we confuse doing for being
And appearing for seeing

So it all appears

No wonder
No wonder.

PART 2

Methods of the Inner Journey

Methods of the Inner Journey – Introduction

Basically all methods lead us to what is already here, to the understanding that everything comes from the same root and that the differences are only appearances. Here in Part 2, I have presented a few approaches to coming here, whether it is a method to be done in silence or in the noise and hustle of a city street, a visualisation, a simple movement or just through looking inside. Some methods may be calming, some may at first bring us into contact with unwanted thoughts or feelings, but all will, if we do them with totality and persist, open up the inner space which is already here and out of which we can live spontaneously.

Awareness Is Perfecting

Awareness is perfecting; it is the constant meditation on what is. We may call what we experience imperfect as the mind always desires more or something different, but the awareness of this 'imperfection' is to perfect the imperfect.

Touching Thoughts

As each breath arises, we touch it or feel its touch. Do the same with the thoughts. Instead of being disturbed or irritated that a thought is coming in your meditation, or in your life at a seemingly inopportune moment, touch that thought. That touch is the beginning of awareness. The habit of moving away from things that don't fit into our plans weakens us, and we turn life into non-life and deaden ourselves.

Practise touching and feeling each thought as you touch and feel each breath. See if you can become aware of the inner jump that happens if you try to move away from a thought, and practise touching this too. It's like when you meet a group of people and you have likes and dislikes – preferences based on how the people look. If you can play by moving around the room together and looking at each other, the differences remain but have been acknowledged and befriended, and then each person is to a deeper degree a part of you. As with people, so with thoughts; when we touch and feel them they are no longer strangers to us.

You may experience that as you touch a thought it disappears, and you return to awareness of breath. This is a parallel to the Advaita anecdote where there is a wedding party with an uninvited guest who can move around and help himself to the food and drink until he is discovered. When someone acknowledges his presence, that is they see and feel him and then ask who he is, then he is nowhere to be found – he has disappeared. The same thing happens in mind: uninvited thoughts, though they may drift by, are not on the guest list but neither do we throw them out. When we just touch and feel them, in a way we bless them and so they take their natural course. The right place for thought is in functional mind, which we explore also, but right now we are practising coming to the ground of being.

Wholeheartedly Invite All Thoughts In

A method that does not expect mind to be silent or create any conflict with mind but, when practised, invites thought in to bring about natural ordering and centring.

When we wholeheartedly invite all thoughts in, then they start staying away, and even when they come we can observe them with more ease, because the wholehearted invitation is a statement of intention and an affirmation of that which is always here. The invitation says, 'Come in thoughts. I am big enough for you,' and when this statement is realised experientially we are no longer in fear of our own minds and our potential actions, because we know we are not the victims of our minds. As the thoughts come and the intention stands to allow all thoughts, then the inner space of awareness is realised, because no thought can fill it. We are that context and we deepen in the realisation that no thought is bigger than 'I', and no thought is who I am.

Identification is forgetting who we are and becoming the thought that arises in our consciousness. When this happens, we are no longer aware of being. In this forgetfulness, there is no longer awareness aware of a thought, but rather the 'I' has become the thought. In this state of mind, it appears that there is no space between who I am and the thought. So the thought is as big as I am, because it is what I identify myself as and hence believe myself to be, or the thought is bigger than I am as in the statement, 'I feel overwhelmed by thoughts.'

Allowing all thoughts is being awareness. Directing attention to the thoughts that arise is seeing them and experiencing them totally. So if a thought decides to come to the party, it must come fully and in its fullness blossom into its true nature. That's a fair agreement. I invite you, thoughts, totally and wholeheartedly and you, thoughts, if you come, come totally so we all show up and let's see what happens together.

Method

Sit comfortably with open or closed eyes. Say silently and inwardly to yourself, 'I invite all thoughts in, without exception.' Sit silently for at least twenty minutes and repeat the invitation when either you find yourself lost in thought or at random when the question spontaneously occurs to you.

Below are possible variations, changing the invitation while following the same basic instructions as above.

With open eyes:
Invite in all you see, without exception.

With closed eyes:
Invite in all you hear, without exception.

With open or closed eyes:
Invite in everything you sense, without exception.

This Too Can Be Here

This method can be practised anywhere and at any time. Whatever you sense, both internally and externally, repeat to yourself silently, 'This too can be here.'

Observe whatever appears in your mind, in your feelings and in your surroundings and continue repeating to yourself silently, 'This too can be here.'

To See Clearly

To see clearly we have to drop 'seeing from' and drop back to 'just seeing', and *feel* the shift back. An example of seeing from is when we have an investment in the outcome of what we see; then we start to see what we think is going to happen or should happen. We see from a thought which anticipates the events and we are not present with what is happening.

Part 1

Say to yourself while looking at anything, 'I see from behind,' or, 'I see from the heart,' or from anywhere else that describes your experience of seeing in that moment. Play with adopting another position to see from, because none is better than any other and they are all as real as you make them. The greater the number of viewing points, the richer seeing is. What will you choose? Which feels clear, deep and whole? Play with the seeing experience.

Part 2

We could also adopt the viewpoint that all things – everything – sees, which means we can therefore be seen and realise: I see trees, and trees see I.

I see you.
You see I.

*

The focus in both parts one and two of this method is in remaining as just seeing and not doing. And if there is any judgement, don't do anything with it, remain as just seeing that there is judgement. Without awareness, what is seen is always distorted by what is being seen through, which are our judgements. A good indicator of the degree of distortion is the degree of disturbance that we experience in any situation, which we can test in the moment by asking ourselves, 'Is there just seeing?' If there is just seeing, there are no ripples of emotion or memory traces or anticipation. For example, if we have a goal but live in constant emotional turmoil, these ripples of emotion distort how we see and we can get lost in the emotions, live in memory or anticipation and get no real feedback from what we are experiencing in attempting to reach our goal. Then we cannot measure our progress towards the goal and the attempts to calm these ripples become our new goals, and so on.

These two exercises in just seeing point towards the state of being, which comes first but is not separate. Hence there is being, which is seeing and experiencing, where being transcends and binds both. Like the apex of a pyramid, which is above all other points in the construction, being is connected and gives expression to all. It is independent of all and at the same time it is dependent on all, because an apex is meaningless without the base and the sides of the pyramid. In pyramid language, without the apex there is no pyramid and without the base and walls there is no apex, but it is the apex which defines the pyramid. The apex is the culmination of the idea 'pyramid'. Conscious being is the culmination of all doing and striving in human consciousness. It also defines us as humans.

How Does Existence Breathe?

Existence creates breath, pretending to make non-existential places, vacuums and empty spaces, and then she enters them. She pretends that these places have no space, that they are tight, limited and dark, and then she brings her wholeness in. The expanse of existence surrounding that seemingly limited and separate non-space enters in. Every time we breathe, we breathe in the whole surrounding space.

Go out into a large open space or look into the sky. Look and feel the vastness of that space. Breathe in and feel the vastness enter and occupy the seeming smallness of the lungs and the body. Allow this feeling, this experience, to expand and deepen with each breath, while continuing to look at the large open space or sky.

Clouds and Space

On an overcast day, look at the cloudy sky. See the clouds. You know there is a sky behind the clouds. You know there is space behind the clouds. See that space – know that space. Now look again at the clouds. Bring together the knowing that there is space and seeing the clouds. See the clouds in endless space.

This can also be done with a dark sky and sunlight. If we climb away from the earth into space we will see the sun and see that it never sets. Awareness also never sets. In daily life, be the space of awareness, see objects and bring both here-now.

This can also be done in social situations. After all, we do feel upset in ourselves at times and have conflicts with others. Can we bring together here-now the knowing that there is awareness and that there are also thoughts which are creating conflict. Can we take a moment to be still and see the clouds and be the space.

Everything Is Here

When I experience the form and the formless, the material and the space it exists in, I experience ...

Everything is here. I am here. What I perceive is here, and all my feelings, emotions and thoughts are here. Where else? But all these are often not experienced as a whole here-now, but rather as a conflict or a flip-flopping, an alternating yes and no to what is. Usually this yes/no goes on until we decide for one side or the other, but this also is not the whole: it is exclusion. When we penetrate the perception, we become aware of the wholeness. When we rest here and experience, through feeling both 'I' and what 'I' perceives, we go beyond perception and 'I'. My perception and who I am merge. My perception becomes me and I become my perception.

The Face Is a Mirror

On seeing a woman, whose face, head and the way she moved it had a moon-like quality.

Method

Imagine and feel your face to be the mirror that is mirroring the world. Let the world touch your face and let your face reflect the world like the full moon reflects the light of the sun.

Tilt your head, changing the angle, like you would when facing the sun on a winter's day when you try to get the position that gives you the most warmth. Open to the pictures of the world. Look around and take in the changing image. Let your face be the mirror on which the images of the world fall and let those images be reflected back.

And let those images be.

And let those images.

A Simple Social Meditation

This is a meditation for those times when you judge your situation and wish you were somewhere else, especially when concerned about the judgement of other people, perhaps in the departure lounge of an airport. Imagine and feel that you will spend the next 48 hours with all these people. Feel and know that you will need to find solutions together so as to live, perhaps even survive, in that time together. Realise that a meditation, like life, is not a calculation or even a consideration, but an act of being which excludes nothing.

The Flow of Conversation Method

Sit in a loud place and listen to the flow of conversation. Living in the middle of life is the ultimate sanctuary.

Finger Exercise

Bring the index fingers of your left and right hands together in front of your eyes and focus your attention on them. Keeping your attention on both fingers, move them apart simultaneously until you can no longer see them.

And then ...

The Heart of the Matter

If you stand and softly, slowly move the chest in and out, you may notice different expressions on a spectrum between powerful, strong and outgoing to collapsed, weak and withdrawn. If a person developed a sensitivity for these expressions and the subtle movements involved, they could find the middle position, both physically and emotionally, and move out of the horizontal into the vertical.

For instance, when we become aware of the space between our shoulders, the natural value of the heart arises and then, instead of the constant effort of pushing forward or contracting the chest, here at the heart we can rest. Here it is not about being this or that: it is the place we are drawn to when we cease to hold on to ideas, thoughts and beliefs about who we are and start to acknowledge THAT we are. That is why I referred to movement away from the horizontal towards the vertical. Just as a stone thrown over a high cliff will at first have the trajectory of its initial direction, after falling for a time it will start to fall vertically.

The falling of a stone and falling inwards are caused by two kinds of gravity: one is the gravity of physics and the other the gravity of Being. Larger bodies draw smaller bodies to them. A person, an expression of a smaller body, is for most of their life on the horizontal trajectory of self-interest and self-motivation. This person will, on letting go of their ideas of who they are – ideas that are even smaller bodies which the person drew to themselves – start to fall in, drawn by the gravity of the greater body, Being, which is who they really are.

Everything is being and, when it is being what it is, it is beautiful, at ease and peaceful. Human beings are being and, when a human being is being what they are, they are one and whole. When we let go of what we thought we were, we are. Once we realise this, it is like coming in from the cold. We have found the fire that constantly burns, so we naturally gather to this and bring all to this. This heart can melt all that is frozen in us and it can bring light where there is darkness and it can be the crucible for the new forms, whether they be words or actions. The heart is all, as it is the heart of all. As we say, let's get to the heart of the matter, and the heart of the matter of the body, including the physical heart, does have a heart. That is why when we are at ease and mind is settled the heart beat slows: the body (heart pump)/mind recognises that Being is and it does not need to do the job of being. The heart pump and the mind are not the life force: they are just functions or servants of life, and when we stand in Being they start to function for us. Everybody knows a quiet mind can approach and complete a task more effectively than a mind stirred up.

Two Hands

The two hands brought together palm to palm are an extension of the arms from the heart. The gesture says, end of action. Only the Heart now – here One. Hands are action. They are symbolic of duality, with left and right and the idea that I can do something. We can be fooled by this and forget and deny the Heart. Bringing the hands together says, I stop and the One here now acts. A simple practice of remembrance would be, while in action with our hands, to remain aware at the place where the hands meet through the arms.

Come Close to Thought

Come close to thought, remaining without definition as awareness.

While looking at any object or person, say silently inside, 'You are I' and direct this thought to the object or person.

While looking at a person or an object, ask yourself, 'Where do I end?'

*

Come close to the thoughts and feelings, as they have something to tell us. We are not aiming to get rid of them: our need is to understand, to recognise and realise. In this method we are not looking to analyse and come to a specific understanding. Each thought, perception or feeling, especially when it often recurs, has something to tell us, because it is a product of our consciousness. This something is not necessarily specific, so we are not analysing the thought; rather we are standing close but not bringing anything at all. We are just remaining present and the understanding is received indirectly as an impression, apprehension, a knowing without a knower.

When we analyse a thought or try to change our thinking, we adopt a defined form as the analyser of the thought. In the same way that the farmer and the property developer, both self-defining thoughts, see respectively arable land and building land in the same valley, any person when trying to analyse a thought will distort what they see through the lens of the analyser, depending on the preferences and intentions contained in their self-defining thought or thoughts. However, if we just remain close to the thought, without forming ourselves into anything but just remaining without definition, as definitionless awareness, then so the thought is also, just as it is, because as we are so the world appears to be, the world being just a reflection of who we are. A person who has an inner conflict is quick to flare up and enter into an outer conflict at the smallest of provocations.

When this approach is understood, new possibilities of mind arise. By being that which I am, the world as a reflection in my consciousness also changes. Previously the idea was that by being something or somebody we could manipulate or dominate the world to make it change. This approach appears to be what keeps people running after something, where each step is a new attempt at change, another thought with the intention of making the world give up what we want.

The deeper a person knows their original nature, the more those qualities of true being come to the world. For instance, when we have realised that all we see is a product of our consciousness, then while looking at a person, an object or a plant, saying silently inside, 'You are I' and directing this thought to the object or person, we can become aware of that reflection in our own consciousness. The act of becoming that which we perceive expands perception to dissolve the division between the one who perceives and that which is perceived.

Another simple application of this approach is, while looking at a person or an object, to ask yourself, 'Where do I end?' While listening to sounds, ask yourself, 'Where do I end?' In touching and tasting, 'Where do I end?' Experiment and apply this to all the senses.

The reflections we sense in our consciousness are our qualities, in the same way that a beam of light entering a prism emerges as the spectrum of colours.

The Re-In-Force or Re the In Force

Reinforce what is real. Give to that which is real and alive. Give 'I' to that which you sense. Give the inner force, the life force in you, to that which you sense. Reinforce what is real.

Give yourself, as 'I', to that which is real. When you see something, bring your inner sense of being, your 'I', to the perception. As you say 'I see' then feel 'I', be 'I' and see as 'I', until there is no 'I' but seeing.

It is the inner force which makes all possible: the inside, the inner. 'I' is inside: we do not search for it outside – that much we know. We don't say, 'I am over there.' We know exactly where we are and when we are. There often seems in some people to be some confusion about who they are, but, if we follow the direction persistently back from over there to here and go on in the direction we are taking, then it becomes obvious who we are. The point is to persist, because without this a person falls victim to conditioning, false assumptions and self-hypnosis or settles for a belief they have been given. Don't stop – complete the path to its conclusion.

I am not over there. I am here. I am not what is here as body and thoughts and other appearances – I am aware of them.

Without body and thoughts, I am?
Without body and thoughts I am …
Without body and thoughts I AM.

The essential force which is inside everything gives life, so give back to life what belongs to life: re-in-force. Use your inner force to merge with the inner force as it is manifested in what you sense. This brings experiential meaning to the statement, 'I am That.'

Each person's 'I' is the individual inner sensing: it is the will, the inner force, the sense of being. Give this to that which makes 'I' possible.

As a variation on this method you can ask yourself, 'Who am I without body and thoughts?' or with a partner practise together, taking it in turns to ask each other, 'Who are you without body and thoughts?'

An Antidote to Dizziness

Method

Whirl – spin around with your arms hanging loosely by your sides for two or three minutes. Stop abruptly. Hold your hand close to your face and look at it.

If you whirl, spin around and then stop, you can stop yourself being dizzy by looking at your hands while holding them still and close to you. If you look at something else, which may also be stationary but at a distance from you, although the effect may be similar it might not be enough to stop your dizziness. The closer the stationary object is, the more effective is its influence in stopping dizziness.

What must this say about the centre of our being, our original nature, our true self, the unmoving, taking into account how dizzy we are in the world, with all these objects spinning around us and thoughts spinning in our minds, and then the centre as the stationary reference point, awareness as the still, unchanging I AM? What an antidote to the dizziness of daily life! When we are aware of that which is closest to us, the dizziness subsides. Even saying 'close' is wrong, because close implies distance and in distance there is movement and the spinning starts again. That which is closest is not even moving.

Perhaps a good definition of a 'thing' is that which moves and comes and goes, which is what happens when we spin, as objects come towards us and go by us. Whereas the original nature, our natural state, could be defined as not coming and going, not being a part of the spinning or the dizziness but close, in fact the closest to us, like our hands, which we can look at when we are dizzy from spinning to alleviate the dizziness. So if we look to ourselves, look in ourselves, we will become centred and the dizziness will stop.

WHERE DO YOU TOUCH YOUR BODY?
WHERE IS IT THAT YOU COME INTO CONTACT WITH YOUR BODY?

Ten Short Ones to Go (IN)

Before Gathering, Gather

Just before the in breath there is a gathering, a subtle, internal, invisible gathering. Watch the breath as if you are dead and become aware of this gathering, then gather in the gap before that gathering. Gather as a non-doing gathering. It is nature spontaneously moving and the formless forming. It is the unseeable appearing. It turns up when we turn down.

Before

IT is, before we have even moved to go searching inside. IT is the seer. Catch that moment before you go to look inside. Or when looking, go back to that place where looking originates. And here find the seer.

On Experiencing Anything or Something

Find the nothingness in relation to that something(ness) and follow nothingness back to its root.

Inside – Outside – Nothing In-Between?

Notice that you can sense, see, hear or touch something outside or you can sense yourself inside, but there is nothing else, there is no in-between. Only these two poles exist, or they don't. If they don't, then all is inside, or if everything is outside the question arises, outside of what or outside for whom?

The outside and the inside are two sides of the same coin – just two different ways of saying the same thing.

What is in, in-between?

What Is This?

Look at something you cannot see
Listen to something you cannot hear
Touch something you cannot sense

Think something you cannot explain
What is this?

Pour Yourself

Pour yourself into that which you cannot fill
Go on pouring and watching

Looking Within ...

... look at that which you cannot see, that which has no form or edges. It is unclear if you are too close or too far away, if this is large or small. You only sense that you see. After that, the deeper you go, the less you are and the more you find.

Looking Out with Closed Eyes

With your eyes closed, look out.
When our eyes are closed and we look out, our eyes converge.
We then look with one eye – it is unavoidable.
We can look into the vastness, totally and single pointedly.
With Closed Eyes Look Out.

Let It Leak

Beyond our knowing consciousness, we don't know.
Beyond what we can describe is the indescribable.
Let this indescribable not-knowingness that surrounds us leak through into our life of knowing.

All and None of It

Pick up an object and put it down
Close eyes
Breathe in that object and breathe it out
Breathe in objects and breathe them out
Is there a clearer demonstration that we are none of this and contain all of this?

Standing in the Doorways of the Senses

Question: What constitutes effective sadhana?

The foremost of all sadhanas is silence of the mind; this is what true devotees should practice.

Bhagavan: Silence is of four kinds: silence of speech, silence of the eye, silence of the ear, and silence of the mind. Only the last is pure silence, and it is the most important.

> *Padamalai – Teachings of Sri Ramana Maharshi*, recorded
> by Muruganar, from Chapter – Advice on Sadhana

When we stand in the doorways of the senses in the mouth and tongue, eyes and ears and in the mind, then we are present as awareness and the sensations normally transmitted grow quiet. Whenever we are present, we become centred and silent.

The intention of this method is to bring experiential understanding to how we make our world and have a direct experience of our true nature. By focusing on each of the senses separately and becoming aware of the specific impressions, we grow in understanding of the process and the components of our sense perception. It is like a sound engineer understanding the components of a certain sound and how it is built up from the bass, mid-range and treble frequencies.

For each of us, our world is a combination of everything we sense reflected in our consciousness. For instance, by being silent in our eyes, in a way we become blind, but actually only then do we start to see. Any previous seeing was just a reaction, a reactivation of past impressions. Likewise, as we become present in our ears, we become deaf to the chatter of the one who makes a running commentary on what is heard, the one who likes or dislikes what is heard. We start hearing what is, instead of hearing the commentary and the interpretation based on past memories. When we bypass this commentary of the mind and experience directly, this commentator, the ego, gets no food and the impressions of the mind, the ego's possessions, which have no permanence and only live like parasites by diverting attention away from the present moment, no longer receive the attention that is their life energy and they wither away. When we bypass the commentating mind using this method, there is less noise or disturbance: we become centred. Because no new impressions are laid down, there is less reaction and, being centred, we have direct experience, as we *are* direct experience. Being aware and present in our mind is being aware and present inside. The one who is not present to the senses becomes a victim of those senses. Then something is seen and the impression shoots into the mind and triggers a memory that has a feeling connected to it, and the mind is in movement, with desire or resistance either trying to recreate the impression that has been laid down in the past or trying to get rid of that same impression.

Check the sense at its point of reception.

Method: Standing in the Doorways of the Senses

Bring awareness to, and stand in the doorway of, the mouth and tongue. Have a silent mouth. Not interfering in the sensations of the mouth, you remain present, silently observing. Have a silent mouth.

Bring awareness to, and stand in the doorway of, the eyes. Have silent eyes. Remain in those two eyes, quietly observing. Not interfering in what the eyes see, you remain present in the eyes. Have silent eyes.

Bring awareness to, and stand in the doorway of, the ears. Have silent ears. Remain in those two ears quietly observing. Not interfering in what the ears hear, you remain present in the ears. Have silent ears.

Bring awareness to, and stand in the doorway of, sensation. Stand in the doorway where sensation appears. Be aware and present with sensation. Not interfering with sensation, you remain present sensing. Remain still.

Bring awareness to, and stand in the doorway of, the mind. Stand in the doorway where thoughts appear. Be aware and present in your mind. Have silent mind. Remain in the mind quietly observing. Not interfering with any thoughts that appear, you remain present in the mind. Have silent mind.

I Am, the Temple

Imagine you are placing candles in your inner space
One candle after another

One candle, another candle
You are placing candles in the temple.

Imagine you are lighting these candles
One candle after another
One candle, another candle
Continue till you have lit all the candles.

Now ask yourself,
From which source did I light the candles?

What Is This Light?

What is this light that shines in the dark interior?
How is it that everything can be experienced inside at the place
of greatest darkness?
What is this light that shines in the dark interior?

To the Light that IS

Go to the place where there are no thoughts and stay there. There
appears to be light outside, but to find the light that does not appear
we need to turn inwards, because there we are that eternal light. The
sun and all other sources of light are temporary. When we turn back
inside ourselves it may seem darker at first, because we travel away
from the light that appears towards the light that is. To do this we
must travel through a twilight zone and through darkness where there
is no light. The light that IS is found through the darkness INside.

Three Sun Visualisation Meditations

(1) Sun above the clouds

The sun is always shining – it never sets. During the winter days in
the north of the planet when it is grey, the sun is always there above
the clouds. Also, when the sun appears to set, it is still there – it is we
who turn away, rotating on the planet, but the sun never sets. Visual-
ise the sun that always shines.

(2) Sun in me

The sun of beingness always shines in me. Little I, the wandering mind, just needs to turn in and see. Turn in and Be. Visualise the sun inside.

(3) Sun all around

Everything is being
Beingness is all around

Visualise the sun radiating from everything.

Walking Above the Clouds

Visualise yourself as standing outside on a day when the clouds are low and heavy in the sky. Imagine and feel the weight of the clouds pressing down on your body. This you can easily do if you remember the feeling of how it is on those days when the body does feel heavier. Imagine this weight. Feel this weight and feel how your body is pressed down to the earth. Feel how the weight bends the back and how it makes you feel smaller, the head dropping forward and the back bending. Do this imagining-feeling visualisation until you can experience it.

After experiencing this for a few minutes, change your imagination and visualise yourself standing outside under the same sky where the clouds are low and heavy, but now extend your attention towards the sky above the clouds and expand your attention-feeling into the infinite space. Extend your attention and imagine the infinity of that space above you pulling you upwards, and feel how your back straightens and how your head moves towards the heavens. Continue extending upwards and visualise that your head is now above the clouds and then the clouds are just around your chest. Go on extending upwards, progressively experiencing the clouds around your waist and then around your knees. You go on extending upwards into the infinite space until the clouds are around your ankles and at times under the soles of your feet. Visualise and feel that you are not tied to the earth but have evolved out of the earth. You stand on the earth, above the earth, but still have contact with the earth. Feel yourself as on the earth, above the earth and beyond the earth.

The Skin Bag Method

In stillness there is vastness; there is no distance as there is no movement. When floating underwater with closed eyes, space simply appears.

When we stop, time stops.

Try it now with closed eyes. Just float inside your sixty per cent water-containing skin bag. Float in the liquid and watch the tides as breath goes in and out.

Being Rubbed Out

Awareness is like a pencil eraser. When we live with awareness, our false ideas are transformed. No matter how much transformation takes place, awareness cannot become stained, as a mirror remains always fresh without a trace of what it has reflected. A pencil eraser, no matter how much it erases, does not remain dirty when we continue to use it. Continued use with awareness is called practice, in whatever method we may use. The proof is in the perseverance of practice.

Try this experiment with a pencil (preferably a soft lead B or 2B), a rubber pencil eraser and a piece of white paper. Make some pencil marks on the piece of paper and then rub them out with the rubber eraser. After a time the rubber may get dirty, but continue rubbing and you will notice that the eraser itself rubs away the pencil residue that had gathered on its surface and the eraser continues to erase. Persisting in the action of rubbing cleans both the paper and the eraser.

When we in our daily lives persist in our action of aware living, there is a self-cleansing and we also remain fresh in the moment. This requires us to be in contact, in the same way that the eraser was in contact with the paper. We need to be in relation to whatever we are meeting, whether it is people, events in the world or our own thoughts and emotions, and then the world and the challenges we face will purify us of our false ideas. We may even notice that the more we give ourselves to the life situation, the sharper we become and the more energy and joy we experience in our doing.

Cleaning, Building, Maintaining

When doing the inner gardening work, pulling out weeds, clearing the ground and cleaning, be sure to plant new seeds, those seeds that we want to grow. Keep the ground clean, be that ground and live from there. Bring order.

Cleaning (inner): clearing, preparing, bringing all the elements into a harmonious natural whole, making sure all elements and tools are available.

Building (outer): applying the insights from cleaning to the outer situation while remaining focused and aware. Creating using the results of insight and understanding as reference and internal feedback systems; so in, out, in, out, in, and so on. On earth as it is in heaven.

Maintaining is the practice of remaining aware of self, other and environment. Honouring those who have taught wisdom down the ages, and passing on the essential understanding through methods, explanations and living demonstrations so as to light the fire in others.

Then maintaining cleaning is the clearing out of the gathering dust of dogma and habit which can develop through repetition. Bringing the freshness of the practice of being present, which naturally is creative and, in the space cleared through cleaning, builds.

Maintaining, cleaning, building.

From Work in Consciousness to Play as Consciousness

If the tools, methods and techniques for playing and working in consciousness on the inner journey are an overlay on our lives, they are the new limiting frame, the new morality, the fenced garden in which we play but we are always inside. The breakout is the return to source. Gather a good understanding of the methods, techniques and tools. Practise single-pointedly in a supportive atmosphere where there is guidance. Then use tools, abuse tools and bend tools until they are the function of being: consciousness at play in life.

PART 3

The Mystic in the Thick of It – Being Human

The Empowerment and Liberation of Sharing and Co-Creativity

Our journey is never limited to us. We may start the journey to alleviate our own personal suffering, but as we progress and deepen in consciousness we become conscious of the world and what is happening around us. Now, being less buried in our own stories, we have more sensitivity and see more clearly, and we start to see how our actions affect others and understand how we as humans are creating together our life on this planet. We are powerful, as powerful as life, as we are life. So let us make a life worth living together on this planet before we destroy it and ourselves through our contributions to global warming, war, famine, the forced displacement of over 65 million people in one year, and the numerous other ways in which we are being destructive.

The heading for this introduction is The Empowerment and Liberation of Sharing and Co-Creativity. Yes, we are co-creating. After struggling with our selves and emerging out of that fighting den, we open our eyes and look around and become aware of our conflict with the world and the possibility of stopping that. For me, it is not enough to sit in perfection and isolation somewhere secluded; having diminished our internal conflicts and come to some understanding about our selves where we are able to see that others are not to blame, we are ready to co-create on a bigger scale and enhance life on the planet. How is it really possible to live in the world but not be of it? Now, in our present world crisis, we are in the thick of it. A great place to learn and create and we will need all the Understanding, clarity and compassion we have discovered in ourselves on our inner and outer journey until now.

This part of the book is to bring attention to how we are living and creating together and through observation and description, both with sincerity and sincere humour, to shed some light on our present situation.

Being Seen and Being Self

The group witnesses and the participant opens to that witnessing. Okay ness at being seen is simultaneously an okay ness of the individual to be.

Being seen is the outer projection being brought home. Okay ness is letting go of the difference between self and other.

Okay ness is dropping the personal differentiation, then what is, is. Allowing what is liberates.

To witness is to allow self and other and to see they are no different. To drop judgement is to be.

The Alchemy of Being Meeting

In a meeting that has the specific intention of enquiring into our true nature, and being that, there is a heightened focused awareness. In the openness of this space, insights arise spontaneously and can be simultaneously lived, bypassing the mind's need to verify or seek confirmation that what is experienced fits into some map or theory of consciousness. This is living on the razor's edge, on the frontiers of consciousness where knowing and not knowing meet. Simply riding the wave, observing where life is going and feeling when something has run its course.

If a person radiates presence they naturally affect others who rise into that presence. Especially if they give attention to the other and speak, they manifest together a field of presence. Through speaking, they add expression to that which, though it cannot be said, can be felt.

For instance, one person said she observed another participant being drama free, just sitting in the seat without walls of protection, and in seeing this she could let down her own walls. There is an energetic communication through radiating beingness and this communication influences how others behave, because presence naturally draws attention and we become that which we give attention to.

A Team – The Same Work and More Energy

In a team, a group of people who have come together for a specific purpose, exhaustion is not connected to what needs to be done. All that needs to be done can be done and more. The exhaustion is connected directly to the resistance to change, and that is connected to where the individual places themselves as an obstruction in the path of the movement to create. Naturally, taking that position requires a lot of energy. Once the individuals who make up the group decide to be channels, as in doors and paths, and active participants in what has been decided, then there is no exhaustion but in fact the same work and more energy.

Appreciation Is Spontaneous

Appreciation is easy: it is a natural response between two or more people who hold the same goal or vision. As they are looking towards a similar goal, they notice when one of them acts to bring that goal closer. Naturally, this is experienced as both personal and collective, and appreciation may be spontaneously expressed in saying, 'Thanks, I see you brought what we are both trying to create closer.' If there is no common goal then actions, like people, are isolated and only personal agendas are operating, even though there may be a superficial pretence of going in the same direction. Then no appreciation can arise, because actions cannot be acknowledged as assisting the common goal. In extreme cases an action that helps achieve the stated collective vision may provoke a reaction, as the personal agenda of another is disturbed, or the action is even perceived to be in conflict with that person's personal agenda.

On Making Mistakes

Have you ever observed the tendency, when experiencing that we have done something wrong or made a mistake, to dive into the substance of the mistake and try to grasp the right way in the hope that, on knowing this right way, the next time the 'same' situation comes along we will have the right answer, action or response? But the same situation never comes along again, and when we react like this we actually miss the opportunity that the situation is offering us.

When we really feel we have done wrong or made a mistake, we do stop.

The thoughts we carry have distorted our observation of the situation and have caused us to make the mistake, so it must be clear that our thoughts are not going to help us. In my experience and observation, what helps is to stop and feel, not to try to get the right answer for next time, not to promise never to do it again, but just to stop. It is this stopping that breaks the continuity of thought, and hence action, allowing us to feel our self-nature – not the wrong self, the one who made a mistake, or the right self who will always get it right in the future – but simply the natural self of being without any compulsion to do or thoughts that things should be different. If we remove all pressure to find the right answer, to promise never to do it again and all permutations of these, then we can stand naked as we are and only that will really help us. Thoughts and promises only clog up consciousness. By looking for new thoughts to approach the situation that no longer exists but we predict will happen in the future, we miss the moment of seeing and Being, the gap, the Holy moment. A good example of this is found in the Zen story, 'Eating the Blame', from Paul Reps' book, *Zen Flesh, Zen Bones*:

> Circumstances arose one day which delayed preparation of the dinner of a Soto Zen master, Fugai, and his followers. In haste the cook went to the garden with his curved knife and cut off the tops of green vegetables, chopped them together, and made soup, unaware that in his haste he had included a part of a snake in the vegetables. The followers of Fugai thought they never had tasted such good soup. But when the master himself found the snake's head in his bowl, he summoned the cook. 'What is this?' he demanded, holding up the head of the snake. 'Oh, thank you, master,' replied the cook, taking the morsel and eating it quickly.

No Man's Land?

An analogy between men's circular stand-up latrines and our personal lives, environment and living space.

In Berlin there are a few antique latrines which are definitely pieces of protected heritage. They are octagonal constructions, so the men urinate on each wall while standing facing outwards. It struck me that the dry land was shrinking, because each new visitor who needed to stand and urinate would stand further back, not wanting to stand in the urine splashes left by previous visitors, and thus the new visitor was wetting more dry land. The effect being that the next man stood back even further, leading to progressive fluid encroachment.

Do the men keep retreating from the urine at their feet until they bump into each other, spinning around only to urinate on each other and then get really pissed off?

Is this a parallel for our refusal to suffer the discomforts of living and relating, and refusing to see ourselves in the other and hence stepping further away from ourselves? Trying to monopolise the dry land, which is progressively shrinking as more people step back, spilling the darkness at their feet – nothing to do with them of course – and the next one who comes steps back again.

If what we see outside ourselves is that which we have decided is not ours or who we are, then that which we reject in this way is made into a shadow. Like the out-takes of a film which never make it to the final cut or the colour-enhancing treatment, it is still rough, lacking in quality because we have removed our life from it. Still, being born from ourselves, it is alive. Now, if everybody steps back in the same way when relating, then in the space between us where relating could have happened there accumulate the rejected shadows, the low-quality, incomplete, failed attempts at being or relating. So the more we spill these failed attempts around us, the more we retreat into ourselves, no longer being alive and connected with all around but becoming isolated, surrounded by a shadow which is bordered by the shadows of others. A zone where shadows are spilt.

So we use and use up the earth and the life we are given. In this way we use life to barricade ourselves in, because what we see outside is not the life we want and we insist it has nothing to do with us. Then everybody needs their island, but at the same time the land available is shrinking, because it has been polluted through rejection and the withdrawal of our attention and basically made uninhabitable. A no man's land without a war going on, just people in a war with themselves, creating the shadow spill zone.

The Floor – A Flawed View

We use our environment both externally through objects and people we try to possess and internally through ideas we carry to create a ground, a floor on which we think we walk, and we identify with this floor as an extension of who we are. After a time we believe this floor to be who we are, but then we have forgotten the ground of our being.

Our home is not a house. Clothes are not the body and the body is not who we are. Clothes maybe nice toys, functional or beautiful but if we don't know the beauty of being they only distract us further from Self-knowledge.

If any floor in the form of belief, customs, social norms, etc., is removed, we think we are falling: falling from grace, falling in social standing or falling in the popularity polls, when actually we are inwardly experiencing falling as we have lost hold of that which we were grasping. But in falling, it is clear that our experience of falling is closer to who we are than the floor to which we had been previously clinging. Clinging or falling for whom? So we can welcome falling. Fall in.

Political Shifts

Political shifts express all the different approaches the mind has to try, through a social situation, to create a good life. The approaches are efforts or strategies to create a good life. All the ideas are attempts, from the micro to the macro, to create a life of satisfaction and comfort. But the swings between the seeming opposite extremes of the political parties and their agendas do not ask the right questions concerning what we are trying to do. All the approaches are 'how to' approaches. How to increase economic growth? How to distribute wealth? How to create equality? How to create peace?

But these 'how to' questions have missed the root question, which is, who are we as human beings? Once we even begin to ask this question, the other questions will through natural progression be answered. Questions such as, why are we here? Where are we going? These are questions for the individual; they are not political and not part of election campaigning.

In elections, questions and answers appear as a choice, where the person voting examines the parties and decides who to vote for depending on how many of their questions are answered. But the problem with this is that there is cultural indoctrination brought about through socialisation and education as to what questions can even be asked. Education acts as a distraction to keep the conversation about the status quo as the only conversation. In education the individual does not feature; the priority is the knowledge to be learnt and the individual is acknowledged only in the event of that person repeating or reshuffling the accepted knowledge, and this leads to very pedestrian progress. The system of education is the intellectual powerhouse of the future for a society and, in its current state, it has a very limited, insular and self-interested view.

A society does not exist apart from the individuals within it, but no society encourages the individual except when that individual agrees with the social norm and becomes a cog in the system, which requires blindness and hence the eradication of that individual. The fact that the essential questions are excluded is an agreed-on and accepted part of the blindness. It is agreed on because the goal of most individuals is a comfortable life and such essential questions are disturbing.

It is accepted that the price of belonging is to adopt the accepted beliefs; to live and speak out otherwise would again bring the individual into conflict with the social norms and this would be uncomfortable. So individuals vote and politicians make promises to those individuals but nobody on either side, individual or politician, asks the question, who is this individual?

Progressive questions from this root question would be:

Who is this individual? Why is the individual here? Where is this individual going and where did they come from? Unless we ask bigger questions, we are dumbing ourselves down individually and as a society. We are putting our heads in the sand, as the ostrich does, and thinking that because we don't see or think anything the existential questions will go away. The questions don't go away. We just go on asking non-essential questions and get non-essential, meaningless answers that we then use to create a society and our lives. Of course, as a result our lives are also meaningless and non-essential, filled with trivia and the latest fashions and trends, and have no depth or roots into our true nature. The only real meaning can be gained through essential questioning, and that starts at the root of who a person is. Who am I?

New Pants

Just imagine if you were to defecate – that means shit – in your pants. You would not consider whether you were the owner of this shit and these pants containing the shit. There is no doubt this is you, your pants, your shit, and the questions of ownership and responsibility do not arise: you know you are sitting in shit – you are the centre of what you experience. So it is clear that all these ideas about ownership and responsibility are smokescreens to hide from ourselves what we already know and what we do not even need to consider or reflect on. To summarise: if you shit in your pants you know it is yours and you don't think about ownership or responsibility. You just clean it up, wash yourself and put on some new pants.

New Pants for Everybody!

So what is responsibility, and is everybody just responsible for their own pants?

Now, just extending your imagination a bit, what if your friend shits in their pants? What is your responsibility?

Where does responsibility end?

Let's pursue this idea of responsibility and have a deeper look. The basic question here is, 'Where do I end?' because that will make it clear. I am at the centre of my life and I respond from here – the response is obvious. When I clean my pants, I serve myself and my health and also the people around me. I no longer have to suffer the discomfort and smell and neither do those around me. So I alleviate suffering by responding to my own situation. The predicament we find ourselves in on this planet comes from desiring to draw a line where this idea of a 'my' self ends and another self begins. If we export chemical waste to be stored in another country, or chemicals that are banned in one country but can be sold in another, then in the short term I am caring for my nation but in the long term we will all suffer, as these chemicals will be released into the atmosphere or enter into the earth and the food chain, which we all share. So the answer is that you and I do not end anywhere, and that is the consciousness we are being challenged to grow into. The shit in your pants might not be in my pants, but if I do not respond to your situation then we will have a health problem which will affect every-body. So I do not end anywhere and ultimately your pants are my pants and we are all sitting in the shit.

Digging Our Earth

If somebody could reduce the cost of deep hole drilling to excavate what is found deep in the earth, because there are definitely useful resources down there, people would dig until they made the earth hollow. Picture it, each country digging their sovereign land deeper and deeper. And where does the sovereign land end? Where does stupidity end? Again, better to drill into your own ground.

Sitting and Driving in Traffic

Everything is suffering. Every thing.

Having a body is like having a car. Once we get into a car and drive out onto the street, we are in traffic, and once we get into the body we get into the mind. In fact, with the body this is more imme-diate: as soon as we are in it the body-mind has started, whereas with a car we have to start the engine and drive off. So life is traffic: we have to follow the rules and we are limited. Once we drive away from the parking place we are in life, in the traffic, and no matter how big, shiny or fast or how old or new our car is we will drive in lines, stop at red lights, get a speeding fine if we drive too fast and a parking ticket if we park in the wrong place or park somewhere for too long.

To get a driving licence, buy or rent a car and finally drive, we will have gathered the thoughts over time that enable us to do this. In the same way, we gather the thoughts of who we are and what life is and step into this idea called 'me', 'my life' and 'my mind', which are one and the same, to learn that all of it is suffering and that we need to learn to sit at the centre of it. We have to sit at the centre of our mind to be free of it and we have to participate completely in the traffic to be free of it. Any thought which thinks it is the watcher of the traffic, that it can dominate the traffic or that it can escape the traffic will postpone the totality of the experience called traffic or life. It is the same in sitting meditation: any feeling will result in suffering when we don't sit at the centre of that feeling. When we sit completely sunken, immersed in the feeling, at the centre of it, then the body becomes bliss and we forget the body. The very act of being in something totally reveals our freedom from it, though outer appearances have not changed. It is the same in traffic when we participate completely, without any idea that it should be different. Then we forget the traffic and we forget ourselves and just get on with life, negotiating the traffic to reach our destination.

When buying or renting a car it becomes our car for a certain period of time and, assuming we are going to drive it, it comes with the rules and the traffic. By identifying with the body, it becomes ours in the same way as the car becomes ours, and we are subject to the rules of the body for this time. This limited period of time we call our life.

I drive in Berlin and I know which routes I can take to avoid the traffic, but when the city is full it becomes clear that there are 'Engpässe' – bottlenecks where all the traffic comes together and there are no more alternatives – and the fact that we are together and driving in lines all the time cannot be denied. It is the same on the motorway: we drive fast, but when we get to the city we have to slow down, and the distance between us and the people we overtook is reduced.

We know all the short cuts, but at some point we get caught. In fear or insecurity our personalities, when they have become too rigid, try to protect us from being here and attempt to control others, to manipulate others into believing certain things, so we get an even bigger reflection of our own illusion until we can't see around the edges and it becomes our reality. Then we suffer, because we believe what we see and don't see what we believe. That is, we are seeing what we have through the filter of our beliefs, but we don't see what these beliefs are. Our suffering is that we leave ourselves out of the process.

That is why, in sitting meditation, the feelings or thoughts that we like and that feel good and the feelings and thoughts that we resist and that don't feel good both bring suffering when we identify with them. Unless we are at the centre of the thoughts and feelings, we are separate from them and they operate exactly in this like–dislike, desire–reject manner. Or put more simply, sitting at the centre of suffering we are at the place where suffering arose, which must be prior to suffering and hence it is not suffering, as suffering has not yet arisen. Here there is no against and no for, but there is still being. This being is freedom from what appears and disappears (whether traffic or thoughts), while at the same time living in what is. Like sitting and driving in traffic or driving in traffic and sitting. So while you drive in traffic, sit. Sit at the centre of the traffic of the mind. Air traffic control without a controller.

What We Appear As Is What We Don't Absorb

What we appear as is what we don't absorb. What others appear as is what we don't absorb.

I was watching a BBC documentary about the greenness of plants, where they explained that the green plants absorb the red and blue photons from the sun and reflect the green ones and hence they appear green. In non-scientific language, that meant to me that trees appear green because they do not take in the green. Or looking at life, what appears is what is reflected, not what a thing has absorbed. Then I realised that human beings operate in a similar way, in that what we appear as is what we don't absorb and what others appear as is also what we don't absorb. What we reflect, reject or won't take in needs to land somewhere, so we throw it out, that is, we project it. Each person sees the reflections of what they will not absorb, or the reflections of that which they refuse to be.

A Reflection on Judgement

The actions we observe in the world are always less damaging than the judgements we hold about them, because we can do something about our judgements but we can't do anything about the actions we observe while we still judge them.

Communication, Communion or Control

Communication has the potential to transform into communion
Communion contains communication without there being two

Where there is an opening, no longer one communicating with
another
Rather one being the catalyst for that One in the other

In communing there is no control
No some bodies to control or be in control
In communication there can be control
When personal investment enters in and it becomes sub-jective
As subjective implies an object
An other

In communing there can be no control because there is nobody
but we
We are not different from each other in essence
In this essence we meet
We meet in Communessence
Let us commence.

Gods as Ourselves Coming Back

A consideration on our situation.

Entertain the idea that the Gods are us, without physical bodies,
in a Godly state of consciousness, observing us as themselves embod-
ied. We are also observing our lives, but are more identified, as we
'think' this is 'our' life. From their position of observation the Gods
have more distance, which makes observation easier. Our close prox-
imity to life makes experiencing unavoidable and it is this experienc-
ing which the Gods desire, because after a while in heaven they realise
they are not moving on as life but are removed from life and that they
are, in effect, dead. As humans our direct conscious contact with life
is our blessing, because life itself is the blessing, not some removed
state called awareness. Awareness is only real when it is in life. Life
is the measure and life is all. Believing in transcending life without
being alive is escapism, anti-life. Anyway, back to the story …

As Gods, we observe ourselves with less identification, but bit
by bit these observers, these Gods, say, 'I'd like a bit more of that,'
or, 'I'd like to really get into that life – it looks interesting,' or, 'I
think I could actually be in life, have a body, be in that whole drama
and still observe it. Yes, I'm ready for a full-blown life with

non-forgetfulness, knowing that it is just a drama on the screen of awareness that I AM, which I choose to identify with or not,' or, 'I'm sure I can ride it without forgetting that I am and becoming identified.'

So one by one these observers, the non-identified, the all-inclusive but exclusive, these Gods, decide to enter into bodies. They become as awareness and beingness embodied in human form and, as all humans, potentially conscious of both their individuality and of the oneness. They are then Being human, human being.

The Nouveau Gods

Taking into account the way society treats animals destined for consumption, with one justification among many being that because we have bred them we own them and hence we have the right to treat them as we wish, then consider how society will treat genetically engineered animals. In genetically engineering animals, those involved in the production will believe they are Gods because, again, they will think they have created these animals and, with this deeper justification and attitude of righteousness, that they can treat them as they please, the animals no longer being seen as living beings in their own right. Unless there is a deeper understanding of, respect for, and honouring of life, genetic engineering of animals or any life forms, including humans, is a recipe for more cruelty.

Culture Passed On through Beauty and Messages

Making a space beautiful, balanced and aesthetic. Giving the land to those who come after in an improved state. These actions carry messages: they say, 'Look, it's important to remember this.' The messages are left in architecture, in paint, in wood, in art, in systems, in decoration, in standing stones and in many other expressions and materials.

Nature has a message. Nature left to be, nature observed and nature shaped – all these when done with awareness communicate the messages of nature to us. Nature communicates to us and we communicate through nature. Nature is also communicating back to us as failed crops or floods. Not only is nature saying, 'Don't be so heavy handed,' because naturally we, being of nature, have something to contribute as guardians, but nature is also saying, 'Listen, look and feel – life takes care. There is no need for you humans to always get involved. Become sensitive and know when to act and when to stop.'

Surrender

Many people's idea of life is, 'First I will get my life together and then I will live.' A life like that is like saying, 'Jane will learn to drive proficiently and then go on the road.' In reality, we learn to drive on the road. We surrender to the traffic and the traffic signs and they, along with the other traffic, indicate where we need to sharpen up and the areas in which we need to practise. In fact there is no practice to driving: there is just driving, and while doing it we immediately get sharper. It is give and take. Eat a bit and use the energy.

To Learn and Leap

To learn to do something, we must watch with total attention that person who knows how it is done, and in watching allow the obvious to hit us. That hit is always right at the centre of our being, because when we desire so much to learn we are at our deepest place. Without any distractions, we are totally here and the spark jumps. Understanding is. Understanding has been gained and many great discoveries made through simple watchfulness of nature.

Take learning to drive as an example. When I grew up with cars I rode in them, constantly heard them on the streets and imbibed the sound of the gear box. When my mother taught a Tanzanian friend how to drive, she realised after a time that he, not having grown up with cars, did not have this gear box sound and rhythm in him, so he had to learn from scratch. Everything is a language which we learn by being exposed to it.

When I first heard electronic dance music, I experienced it as monotone. As I listened to it, danced to it and played it, the music went deep into me. I allowed it to enter me and occupy me and I learnt the language. That language is a limitation like any language. These limitations imposed and followed, like rules, form the limits which everybody adheres to and creates within. As the limits are respected, a body of work develops, and then as these lines dictated by the body of work become clearer they can also be broken, in steps wherein the original works, like traces or triggers, can still be recognised. That was the genius of Jimi Hendrix: he broke the rules, but he was so deeply steeped in the tradition of rhythm and blues and the techniques thereof that he could take large leaps, but still the roots could be heard or felt. He was so deep in the tectonic of the electronic, where the lava shifts the plates, flowing but appearing at the surface to be taking rupturing but rapturous leaps which are still settling into the aesthetics of the musical culture. The culture has not digested him, and this is demonstrated by the fact that people copy him but nobody goes beyond him. We can only really use and extend that which we have truly digested and made our own.

Our Desire for Comfort

In all our outer exploration, from simple carriages to move across the earth's surface up to space rockets, we want to travel – or better to say, in the case of space, we need to travel – without being touched by or exposed to the environment we pass through. We desire, in all forms of long distance transport, to not be affected by the journey, and we continue to develop our vehicles for this reason. We call this comfort or luxury. Soul is exactly that: it is the perfection of the vehicle we travel in or as. The purer it is, which means the less it is attached to and influenced by phenomena it encounters, the further and more persistently it can travel back to its source, to that which it is the finite form thereof. So comfort in cars is good, but we should not forget the inner journey and the effortlessness that is naturally ours as we ease into our soulfulness.

The deeper the soul, the stronger the will, but not our will.

Action, Time and Rhythm

When we perform actions that relate to specific periods of time, we become more aware of these periods and we stand in these periods, for example when we water plants and notice the rhythm connected to them. Because certain plants need to be watered at specific intervals, when we postpone or forget that timing we damage the plant. That timing is also lost to us and we have missed the teaching the plant had for us. This teaching applies to all aspects of our surroundings, including our bodies, friends, work, nature and animals. A simple example is how we walk differently on dry or wet ground, uphill or downhill, in daylight or at night. These are all adjustments we may take for granted, but if we become sensitive and aware of them we can see how this makes us more aware of the landscape through and over which we are walking. Developing consciousness in this way helps us move more harmoniously in relating to others, or in a crowd or traffic, or in how we share the planet with all our fellow beings.

Spiritual Institutionalism

The Spiritually Institutionalised person waits to be told what to do, and then they rebel, react, blame and accuse. They think they are so free and so special being in their group with their Teacher or Master, but they have indoctrinated themselves about what they consider to be freedom and hence they are always under threat from Truth, which does not care for their ideas. Freedom after all cannot be contained in anything – that is the nature of freedom. So the Spiritually Institutionalised person goes on trying to get it right, trying to possess and monopolise understanding according to their viewpoint or the imagined viewpoint of the group or teacher. But this viewpoint is just a signpost pointing towards freedom and it isn't itself free or freedom. In this way the Spiritually (self-)Institutionalised person creates their own prison out of a teaching that potentially could have liberated them if they had looked where the signpost was pointing. But they would rather, because of their own defensiveness, go on solidifying their mind a little each time they contract. The positive side to this is that, in this dilemma, feeling threatened can actually be healthy if simply felt, because the attention then moves from the thought towards being-feeling, from head to heart, from rigid consciousness back to flowing consciousness.

Where this Spiritual Institutionalism exists, there is limited authenticity, because the institutionalised person is always trying to get it right or to remember and follow the party line, so they are mostly referring to memory in what they see and in how they react. They always have an answer and miss the point that they are themselves the answer, so most of their behaviour is borrowed. By borrowed behaviour I do not mean actions, disciplines and rules to be followed to maintain community and practice, but rather borrowed robotic behaviour which carries their contraction, as opposed to carrying their flavour as the intelligence and attitude they bring to their actions. Listening to a person when they speak authentically we learn from them, in that moment imbibing their being and viewpoint. A Spiritually Institutionalised – read here also indoctrinated – person does not adopt this attitude. They cannot, because their mind is full of thoughts on how they should act and speak to preserve and protect the institution of, and in, their mind, where they have built their position and their security. Even if they are suffering from this security, as in living in a high-security prison of their own making, they prefer this to feeling, being and not knowing. These qualities of feeling, being and not knowing are for me the basis of relating and communicating, which are vital for any transmission of teaching to take place.

This brings me to the purpose of this writing, which is to bring to your attention the possibility of you actually participating, without the compulsion of Institutionalism, in this relating that for me has become the natural form of this teaching. After all, we can Understand, Awake, be Still and Know but, from my perspective, without relating this is dry: there is no juice, no humanness, no poetry or prayer and definitely no Godliness in it.

Perhaps this speaks to you and you find yourself in what is written here.

The Summit of Senselessness
(German Title: Zusammensein in Unvernunft)

Too True to Be Good

If you have come to realise that trying to be good for God, or whatever your projection of authority and perfection is, has not brought you the reward you were promised, you might be ready for *The Summit of Senselessness*.

The *Summit of Senselessness* has been described as off the wall, so if you are still sitting *on* the wall of your life watching life go by, to finally be off that wall will bring clarity as a direct experience to what you are doing.

Marketing by the Gathering of Fools

Don't get me wrong – the fool is a most desired character in my book. We need more fools. Not idiots, but fools. Fools have a willingness to be from the inside out; they are not so concerned about how they look and hence they are free from all looks and judgements. They give everybody the opportunity to look, and hence are liberating people from the prison of looking away, firstly from themselves and secondly from life. Fools are liberating people into the life that is going on in them and around them. The world needs more fools. Fools to speak out and fools to shut up. Fools to write books and fools to risk saying it how they see it. Singing it how they see it and dancing it how they see it. More dance, more dance.

A Gathering of Fools would be a true place to be, a place of intimacy, sincerity, playfulness and a place of healing, as each person's beauty and creativity that has been buried would have space to spontaneously emerge. A fool's discipline would be just being. Simply fluid, transcending any ideas of how, where and when to be. I am that fool, though to say such a thing is the height of foolishness, but still … Maybe I am speaking to other fools who know in their hearts what I am speaking about. I know it is worth it.

PART 4

The Enquiry – How Far Can You Go?

Self-Enquiry – An Introduction

Through Self-Enquiry (Atman Vichara), enquiring, 'Who am I?' or variations on this question such as, 'For whom does this thought come?' or, 'From where does this thought arise?' the false is seen for what it is, as ideas and concepts which we take ourselves to be, and when the false is seen the real becomes obvious as that which does not come or go. Simply put, the practitioner follows whatever thought arises back to its source and, in the same way as we affirm our selves and know we exist, it must be this reality we are referring to as 'I', as this comes before all thoughts, including the root thought 'I'. Hence the term 'real I' or real-i-sation, where the real is the ground out of which all else arises.

The pieces in this section look in different ways at this method, straying way beyond the traditional approach and then returning, while 'I', thought, self, ego, action, etc., are investigated and even a sofa couch has Buddha nature.

Ramana Maharshi encouraged the use of Self-Enquiry as he said it brought immediate results for the practitioner and this was an encouragement to persist. It is a method of using mind to go beyond mind, and Ramana often described the Enquiry as using a thorn to remove a thorn in the foot, after which both thorns are thrown away.

Ramana taught the Enquiry continually through his lifetime, so any of his books will give you a deeper explanation of this approach. Please note that when I use the word Enquiry with a capital E in this book, I am referring to this method of Self-Enquiry.

The Search

As all we value and desire, including Understanding, Peace, Love, Attention and Life, comes out of who we are, why not know who we are and through THAT know all that comes out of us without having to go searching for it?

Watcher Consciousness

The watcher consciousness, which is conscious of something, arises with that thing and we call this consciousness 'I', as in I see, I hear, I feel, I … Well, you can fill in the gap. And that is what we do: we fill in the gap, the space where being is.

'I' is conditioned consciousness. Consciousness is conditioned by what it is watching, observing. A condition of its existence is its being conscious of that thing. If there is no thing, consciousness also does not exist. Imagine, right this moment, all that you are experiencing drops out of your field of perception and you will get a taste of what I am saying.

'I' in this sense is also a thing, so two things arise together. 'I' is limited to the arising of objects in awareness. If nothing arises then why should 'I' bother to arise, or if nothing arises how can 'I' arise? The 'I' and the object arise together, simultaneously. If another, called 'you', does not arise, what purpose does 'I' serve?

Clearly there is a great insight into oneness here in that you call yourself 'I', and for this 'I' a 'you' arises, and for that 'you', which was present before you named it and naturally calls itself 'I', a 'you' also arises, which is you, but you call yourself 'I'. Different but the same – or not real?

At home alone we are just being ourselves and then somebody else appears and we become somebody. Then we are no longer alone, as in all one, but we have split into 'I' and that which we wish to present to the world, or to the other, 'you', who has appeared. So subjectively we say 'I' and objectively, towards any other we perceive, we say 'you', but really they are all the same. The funny thing in this game is that people do not know the subject, so they are mostly busy with the object, but when the subject is known both the object and the subject drop out of the game. 'I' and 'you' are the same or 'I' and 'you' do not exist, but they do, and that is the game we enjoy playing, or not.

Approached in this way with this understanding, the question, 'Who am I?' is effortlessly answered in the very experience of being. Not thinking an answer and not contemplating, but direct experience.

The Light of Self

The light of Self or the light that lights all lights is not limited. To think it is a light is already a limitation; better to just think IS, and it is this ISNESS that makes everything possible.

That am I. And know that THAT does not become less or more at any time.

This means that if an individual has success and is rewarded financially or with praise, THAT does not become more. Nor if there is failure or loss in any form does THAT become less.

Ask yourself when there appears to be loss, like when you missed the bus, did YOU become less? You got the job, a raise in salary. Did YOU become more? You lost your wallet with the money you had just taken out of the cash machine. Did YOU become less?

Now this can lead to passivity if not really understood, so we need to pay attention. As THAT, although you never become more or less, you do shine, you radiate, but that radiating is not a doing – it is the nature of Being. This radiation is like the sun: although it does nothing, it nourishes and growth happens. This is liberation from the personal to the Real. The personalised light thinks, 'Me, my light. This is me. I am shining.' In liberation or Understanding, light just shines and this shining is by no means passive.

It is like fossil fuels: they are trees which have imbibed and been soaked in the sun. They are only condensed sun and they owe their being what they are, and the power and light they give, to the sun. Alone they are nothing. All individuals, all beings, have as their source the Self, Being, the essential nature without which nothing can exist. They have imbibed and are permeated with Being, with Self Nature. Hence there is cat nature, tree nature, human nature, etc. Just as a fossil fuel such as coal is trees that have been compacted under extreme pressure and become dense, the differing natures of cat, tree and human are only compacted spirit or condensed essential nature, and they owe their nature, their being what they are, to Spirit: alone they are nothing. And Spirit, even in this density as form, is still free, in the same way as we all experience our bodies ageing but inside we don't feel ourselves to be different.

Self Is Not Localised

Self is not localised; if it were it would be a result of, and dependent on, certain conditions and situations or physicality requiring certain physical constellations or the need to adopt certain postures. But if we believe that these circumstances and physical conditions bring about the result, and that resulting experience is something we call our self, it is not beyond calling and as such it is not Being.

Self IS and that is the beauty of the Enquiry, as it starts directly with you now pointing at the Self, asking, 'For whom does this thought come?' It is a direct action and a path for direct experience. The question does not ask us to do anything else and there is no suggestion of an answer, because you look and realise what IS.

Self or Awareness, being always present, is not coming or going or changing, not waxing or waning, so it is beyond form. All names are associated with degrees of a quality or a material, but Self IS and hence has no degrees, no name or form. Being formless, it is not a result of a combination of forms, nor does it have locality in which it arises. We can say the reverse, that locality arises in the Self, but not that Self has locality. Forms are combinations of different elements in space.

Water is hydrogen and oxygen, and the product combined in the right environment and quantities, two molecules of hydrogen to one molecule of oxygen, is water and the process can be reversed. But the Self is source: it is the root, it remains Self and source, and all forms arise in it, but it never rises or falls as it IS. Unlike water or any other combination of elements, you as Self are not reversible. Try unSelfing yourself or try to deny that you exist.

From Forest to Garden

Following a thought back to where it arose from is to develop familiarity with the inner terrain. Now instead of being a forest it becomes a garden. Each time you walk through your garden you get to know where each plant is, you find new ways, you see what could be trimmed. Basically you give to the garden the flavour of awareness. Consciousness then is no longer wild and flickering with each gust of wind, but rather it burns steadily.

Weaving Thoughts and Silence

Each time we follow a thought back to where it came from, we are taking the thread of the thought which was loose and hanging out of the cloth and weaving it neatly back into the cloth of our true nature.

A Thought to End Thoughts

If a person can, on seeing a random thought arise, address it as 'a thought', that thought has no more power – it is meaningless. In the same way that when you take a taxi home your address has meaning – it is the concept which gives the driver the direction – but once you are inside your house the address is meaningless. Or a postal package carries your address and is delivered, but once you receive the package the address has no meaning. The address only has meaning at a distance. When the goal to which the concept was pointing has been reached, the concept no longer has any meaning. I am speaking here to people who want to go home, to source. At source, all talk about source or ideas masquerading as source are seen for what they are – pale copies or pretenders.

See the point – a worry, a conflict, a story and a person all start with a thought, and if that thought is not seen for what it is then thoughts accumulate, and birds of a feather flock together. As more thoughts accumulate, they get denser and a person forms, a situation, a world, etc., like bricks constructing a building. If, on the other hand, the thought as it arises is addressed as a thought, which is all it is, then this process stops and is reversed. The dense accumulation of thoughts starts to disperse and lightness appears where before there was heaviness, because now with fewer thoughts or without thought there is space, and it is this space or ease that all beings long for, as it is our True Nature. As the nature of energy is to move, the energy that would have been tied up or solidified into a person then becomes free and moves. Try this and remain aware of this movement.

A Sofa Has Buddha Nature

Sitting meditation or the practice of awareness is sinking down through what we appear to be, to reveal who and what we are. In the same way that muddy water clears when left undisturbed, so the misunderstanding about who and what we are – our mistaken identity – clears when mind is left alone and just observed.

For instance, if a sofa couch had consciousness (which it does) and just remained as a sofa, meaning it stopped listening to all the conversations of the people sitting on it, stopped identifying with those people and their moods and positions as they sat on it (the sofa) and rather – preferably when empty but not necessarily so – sunk into itself just as it was, a sofa, then without a doubt it would realise its sofa nature. As is clear from the metaphor, this process requires that a sofa is conscious of itself and others. This consciousness is both a blessing and a tragedy, because it is this consciousness that enables the conscious being, or enables that which has consciousness, to forget itself and identify with something else. But it is this consciousness which also enables this being to return home, out of the maze of mistaken identities or illusory selves. This experience of being lost is vital for learning to sift through and sort out the false, developing discriminatory powers, and hence using this function of consciousness as opposed to being used by it and stumbling blindly from one mistaken identity to another.

The 'I' in the form of the discriminatory intellect, though useful, then also comes to an end when it dissolves into the Self, because it encounters something which cannot be taken apart. The 'I' of the intellect being absorbed in the Self, which has no duality, has become one with Self and hence loses its discriminatory powers. When all is the Self and oneself and concepts no longer function or have power over what is, then the opposites collapse. After all, it is only the intellect which says up or down, right or wrong, big or small: in Reality there is no such thing. Try going very close to a so-called small object. It becomes very big, so big that it can block out the sun which is the source of all light on the planet and in our vast solar system. A grain of sand in your eye feels big because it disturbs the means of seeing with the eye; the same sand grain when out of the eye is called small. So, clearly, it is all relative to position. The concepts themselves have no power, only the power we give them. The dual is in no way in conflict with the non-dual.

Thoughts Go to Loam

Thoughts are like a dry crust on the garden soil, a crust that acts as a barrier. When we go in and follow thoughts back, turning the dry crust of the soil, we take thoughts into the loam, into the fluidity of the earth and into the fertility of our nature. As these thoughts, whose whole existence depends on their being separate, enter into the organic natural interconnected whole, they dissolve and become their essential creative nature.

We Think

We think that we suffer because we are here and then want to get there. The reality is we suffer because we are not here.

Be the Target

Thoughts appear from seed
Find the core
Penetrate
Drive into them

Be the target

Breath and Thought

Breath and thought occupy the same place
Their absence is presence

Each Thought

One can ask of each thought directly, 'Where do you arise from?' This is also a form of penetrating the thought to that which is the seed of all thought. As the thought is penetrated to its seed, which is the 'I' thought, that which is before 'I' and before thought is realised.

(Imagine an image of bubble-like forms with seeds at their centre. The essay later in the book entitled Surface Tension looks more deeply at the theme of the 'I' thought as the glue or the tension holding together all the bubbles and the forms the bubbles create.)

Only So Far Good Friend

When following a thought back, there is only so far the thought can go. Like putting objects in a fire, paper burns more quickly than wood but wood also eventually burns. A thought's natural home is not at source: thoughts live and operate on our periphery where they are useful for functional activities but not for essential living.

Why do we need to put anything in between ourselves and the world of objects or phenomena?

Because we don't know the nature of our existence, and in not knowing it but still vaguely sensing it we try to create it using what we think we know, which is using all we have learnt and been told. But these resources and the motivation to try and create our true nature are already doomed to fail because they leave out the obvious, that we already are that true nature and we just need to look a bit closer to home and subtract what it is we are adding.

That Inward Look

Any idea we could have about who we are or what Self is or looks like is another distraction from the inward look. When we stop at any object or thought, we are already looking out, because these ideas or thoughts are always on our periphery. To look in and be whole, our totality of attention needs to be brought to that inward look.

Willing to Experience Emptiness

When we go on jumping from one thought or belief to another, perhaps believing we should know or believing we should be this or that, we basically believe that we have to be some-thing when we aren't a thing. If we watch mind and our actions closely we realise this, and we see that the effort driving it all is a part which appears and disappears, so clearly it is not who we are, and it requires a lot of effort to keep up the pretence that it is who we are. When this pretence is seen, the question may arise, 'Well then, who am I?' and that is the start of an effort to discover the Real. That is Right Effort in the Buddha's teachings, which is directed towards realising through deepening and stabilising in what we Understand, Know and feel ourselves to be as a direct experience. When we are willing to experience the Emptiness, the mystery, the not knowing, then we will stop jumping from one thought or belief to another and remain present, being aware of the context. Awareness aware of itself: for short we call it Self, That which we are, in which all of this is appearing to appear and appearing to disappear.

Unlimited Supply

Normally we define ourselves by the content of our minds, but if we are just single-pointedly looking within we can look beyond the content. In the same way that if we wanted to look as deep into space as we possibly could, we would see that there are planets but we would look beyond them. Looking beyond anything is a form of deliberate blindness and we do it all the time in our selective perception. When we go into a supermarket we know what we want and everything else falls into the background until what we are shopping for jumps into the foreground. Now, having the intention to find what we are by looking in is easier than knowing what we want in the supermarket, because what we are *is* already. In going shopping, what we want may be out of stock, but what we are is never in short supply – we have it within us at all times.

The background to all content and experience is always present, but we normally ignore it. The background is our source and it is our existential foundation. It is where we come from and return to, and also at the same time never leave. We are pure and impure simultaneously. Perfect and imperfect at the same time, because as we appear from awareness we take on forms which are certain aspects or expressions of consciousness, so we are a defined part. But at the same time we *are* still holy, whole and one with source because we can do and be nothing without that connection to the foundation or substratum.

To look in and Understand is to turn this habitual way of defining ourselves through the content of our minds upside down and inside out. It is to see that we are consciousness having an experience through the content. We dress ourselves up in clothes but return to who and what we are, without clothes, when we rest at night.

The Deception

Being at first glance looks like nothing. Original nature or the natural state is so obvious and always here that most people don't apply themselves or persist to look, see and realise what is actually here. Original nature contains the qualities people admire and seek. Except that people seek these qualities in things, in experiences, in feelings, sensations and in stories. It is like when you stop drinking sugared drinks and start drinking water. At first water seems tasteless, tastes of nothing, but water is the element in all the other drinks which makes hydration possible and it is the carrier for them all.

No water, no coke. It is the same with the experiences we seek: we will see that they are all grounded in the natural state when we stop and look. The natural state is the carrier. From here we can see more clearly what we need to function, because it is not about dropping out but about dropping in and then, through seeing, dropping out of games or dropping what is unnecessary.

Consciousness – The Inner Force

When there is attention on something, this can feel safe and known, but as we go deeper and become conscious of the root of what is happening we see there is awareness. Firstly and always, there is awareness. This is not such a known territory, or perhaps I should say it is not a territory of knowing, as it has no objects to be known by. It is awareness before objects. Here a person is alone, as there is only awareness. This awareness is like a flame, and everything else is secondary. First comes the flame of awareness, then comes the light of consciousness, and then comes the object. The unfolding or ordering is first awareness, next the light of awareness which we call consciousness, and then the focused directed light of awareness called attention, and then the object sensed by that attention. In this there is both consciousness sensing the object and awareness aware of itself. This is non-dual perception, Oneness, as that which sees and that which is seen are in Awareness and are of the stuff of awareness, the Self.

In this unfolding there is distance, space, inclusion, presence and awareness of consciousness.

Before this is understood and experienced, what is seen is taken for granted, assumed to be, and in this assumption there is dullness. In consciousness there is aliveness, because this is the root of attention and it is this which makes sensing and perception possible. As with a river, without its source it could not be. The source of the river is its aliveness, its most pure form.

I was observing a child of about six weeks of age being held on its father's arm, over which it was looking in my direction. It was a summer's day in a park next to a playground and there was a lot of sound and movement, quite a lot of impressions for a newly born child.

I noticed the child made movements with its head while at the same time opening and closing its eyes. It seemed to me that the child was using its will to position its head in the direction of what it wanted to see. The child appeared to go on adjusting its head and the lenses of its eyes, all actions performed to create the right perception. And when the perception was satisfactory, the baby just stared and took in the scene.

I could observe will in action, will positioning the head and then will adjusting the lenses in the eyes. This was the inner force manipulating the physical apparatus. The baby was aware of itself: it clearly felt its definite beingness and had become aware of another. It then seemed to use its will to bring order to this 'other' which it was sensing, through head positioning and lens focusing. Once the definition of that something else was focused, the baby stopped and observed. This I believe is the inner force of consciousness, using the physical apparatus of the body.

Lookers and Finders or Burn Up and Being

Looking for the 'I' is like looking for the exact place where a space ship, returning to Earth, passed through the atmosphere. Concepts and calculations can come up with some coordinates and a relative construct, but nobody can indicate the place, because the Earth's atmosphere spins and our calculations cannot catch time and space. You can't step into the same river twice – Heraclitus was right.

In the same way, you cannot find yourself and you cannot find where you are, because you are. It is in the real finding that the logic of analysis ends.

The real practices of enquiry and inner search burn up the one who is doing the looking and wants to find. The one who is looking will have to go if real finding, which is Being, is to be realised. A looker or a finder would be a product of its own source. To continue the spaceship metaphor, it would be like a space research vehicle becoming self-aware and autonomous, coming back to Earth and, while having its data collection downloaded by NASA, simultaneously sending a message to NASA saying, 'I have discovered humans and they are now investigating me.'

So it is nonsensical for lookers to expect to be finders of themselves, partly because lookers aim to find and not to be and their source *is* being. Still, there is finding, and it is this paradox that logic cannot hold but beautifully, liberatingly, it is so.

Practising to be that which IS burns up the false, burns up that which is trying to be, or pretending to be. By immersing ourselves again and again in that which is, we become it in every molecule of our body, perceiving it as life, aliveness, a vibration, a direct experience, a direct current of the Self.

Not 'I'

The action of addressing experience as 'not I' undoubtedly leads to a direct experience of true nature. Each thought, when you don't realise it is not who you are, is you planting a false seed in the womb of your consciousness or letting a cuckoo into your nest. So don't be surprised when the cuckoo flies and you, having brooded over the idea, gestated and given birth to it, are identified with it and then you fly too, having forgotten who you are.

Each thought has as its root the 'I' thought, and when we as the guard of the temple let an impostor through we fill the temple with false Gods or false mythologies. We idolise the ego, we worship our world of thoughts, and this hijacks all our energy and attention. It is the world and the ego and has never satisfied anybody, because we become its captive and it never gives what it promises, but our belief that it will and our worshipping of thoughts and beliefs keeps us dependent.

Practising, 'This is not I' is reminding yourself that this is not who you are, or in other words re-Minding. What could be left but who you are? But then, this is not a thought nor a collection of thoughts called knowledge – it is Knowing.

The words written here in themselves are empty unless a person applies them now. Only the application, the practice of this, brings results. Try it and see and as they say in Zen, 'Practice is Enlightenment.'

Looking for the 'I'

Searching for the 'I' when a person enquires, 'For whom does this thought come?' is like the harbour police seizing a large delivery of counterfeit goods. There they are, standing in the warehouse or on the docks waiting for the people who were supposed to take the delivery, and nobody turns up. Valuable stuff with customers waiting to buy it, but nobody takes delivery, and it is the same with this elusive 'I'. Normally, thoughts come and somebody takes delivery, this somebody we call 'I'. Yes, normally, when the police are not swarming all over the warehouse, the dealers come and pick up the consignment of drugs or stolen goods.

Look – let's be clear – nobody is a thief or a criminal. These people are just doing their job. If you ask them, they say this is what they do and they have good reasons in themselves for doing it, as does the 'I' who covers all reasons and purposes for its existing. Nobody, if the police ask them, is a criminal. Nobody. And nobody is 'I' if you ask, which means nobody takes delivery of the goods, which are the thoughts. The goods or the thoughts are only received if the police are not there, or if nobody is asking who takes delivery. Similarly, thoughts are stolen goods, and they are only received if we become unconscious. People forget themselves only when they are distracted by the desire to be something or to get something, or if the fear of being nothing gets so strong that they cannot bear to do without a thought fix* or a thought to fix them.

Now if the police lay low, out of sight, they may draw the criminals out of hiding. Even if the criminal knows the police are there, he may take a risk; after all, the goods are valuable and he can make a good profit from that delivery. Perhaps that would make a good story line for a sadhana crime thriller. Send me my cut. So why not take the risk? It might work out. And it's the same with thoughts: to take delivery of them, you need to take delivery of the 'I' thought, in other words take on a false identity and lie to yourself that this is who you are and that these thoughts are valuable and that they can give you something. Only in ignorance of the real currency do we go on collecting counterfeit currency. Once we know something is false we stop treating it as real.

*Thought Fix

A thought fix is a thought to fix you up
And it does
It stitches you up
It suspends you
It fixes you in time
So while all else flows, you stick.

Know No

Know
When you no
Then yes.

The False Presenter Can Be Let Go

When practising meditation and observing that there are thoughts, we may become aware of the strategies of the 'I', which is also a thought, now posing as a meditator where it adopts a position in relation to what it observes. And, very importantly, if this observer, the meditating 'I', encounters a thought or feeling to which it cannot find a position, it goes into sleep, confusion or total identification. These strategies are based in the ground rule of self-preservation. In this action of self-preservation, we choose the position to observe from within which we look strong, good and right, the position that will affirm and preserve who we think we are. Then, when a thought or feeling is experienced as being too strong, the observer, the meditating 'I', has to position itself in relation to the thought in such a way as to maintain its existence. So rather than widen out, feel uncomfortable or observe its own demise, the ego-I, or observing self of the meditating 'I', chooses its default program, which is, 'I don't exist,' in the form of sleep, confusion or total merging/identification with the thought/feeling. These are all anaesthetics, but the real practice of meditation is one of removing all sleep: it is awakening to who we are and being aware of what is happening in the moment it happens.

More understanding and awareness can be brought to this process through using the method in Wholeheartedly Invite All Thoughts In, or through holding the 'I' as the separate observer from the summary of Identification Is the Nature of 'I'. In both methods, when practised, the ego's escape mechanism cannot function and ultimately the 'I' is seen for what it is. It is an appearance, something that comes and goes, which has been falsely presenting itself as who we are. In this seeing we can let it go.

How Far Can You Go?

In the film *The Matrix*, the code of the matrix was a computer program of numbers and symbols scrolling continuously, so the matrix, the experience of existence for the people in the matrix, appeared to be continuous. The stream of thoughts and the patterning of consciousness are the same: thought after thought without a gap. Even gaps become thoughts because we call them gaps or, because we cannot conceptualise them, we do not recognise them and hence they do not exist for us. Our minds fill the gaps because the ego, which is the root thought of all thoughts called 'I', has precisely the function of filling through labelling the Reality of Awareness, as it believes itself to be labelled 'I'. The ego knows that without a definition it does not exist, so it is just performing its job and being true to its nature by filling through labelling and defining and hence reproducing the image of itself in all it encounters. But who we are is not defined: we are the definitionless awareness where all this filling, defining and labelling is happening. It is only through our being awareness that this can happen, so don't be too hard on mind and ego – they are just doing their job, in the same way that water flows and wind blows. They mean no evil and they do no evil. The responsibility is ours when we identify with them and their spinning, in the same way that we are responsible when we allow how we feel to be dependent on the weather.

After thoughts, the next level is feeling, because we can stop all thoughts by holding one thought and then find the one who holds that thought. This one is called 'I' as in, 'I hold the thought X' and below this is feeling because, just as all thoughts carry with them a feeling, 'I' also has a feeling. Each of us knows we are, and the word 'I' never sums up who we are, but we know we are because we feel we are. This feeling seems to be the net, the continuity. I always feel 'I'. I AM always my Self, I. I am all ways.

We live in a feeling-being existence that we call life, where even non-being is life, as all is potential and nothing is removed from the source and nothing is devoid of life force as its origin is life. We have moved from thoughts, the Matrix stream, perhaps often feeling overwhelmed by and not in control of the thought stream, to finding that we can hold a thought and stop the stream, because the source of 'I' does not move, in the same way that the wheel spins but the centre of the wheel does not move. So if we watch any movement we can go beyond it and realise our centre. Realising this centre is recognising that this holder of thought, or beholder, exists and is always here. This is what it feels like to be alive, and it is the Being out of which the thoughts arise. The environment and our relating are Being being in infinite varieties and responding to itself, so there is nowhere Being is not. In fact our relating *is* our environment, as we cannot perceive an environment without being aware of it; hence our environment is just an extension of that awareness, I am.

How far can you go?

Our relating is the interface that we are aware of, so the deeper our awareness, the more sensitive we are, the more related we are and the bigger our being is.

How far can you go?

As we are already limitless, we are just reclaiming, rediscovering or uncovering, from under a seemingly continuous stream of thoughts and the debris of memories, that which we already are.

How far can you go?

How far can you go?

How far can you go?

Capturing Space

Capturing space is contemplating emptiness, the fullness-emptiness-potential.

So capturing space is grasping the invisible, is digesting God and is to know, become and BE. Die and be digested.

'I'. Identities as Sticks

The 'I' concept, the one who we think we are, is a collection of ideas, but if we see them for what they are the construct slowly loses strength and with that the seeming power to dictate to us. Strange to see that that which we call ourselves, 'I', the one (or many) who tells us what to do, is actually not who we are but an impostor.

Having accepted all these ideas, we have hypnotised ourselves and been conditioned by society to believe this is who we are. Naturally 'I' tells us what to do: I listen to myself, each person follows himself and so it should be. But if this 'I' is not who I am, then what? Then at some time we will need to confront the impostor.

Picture 'I' as a stick, which in many ways it appears to be. In the English language, even the word 'I' is shaped like a simple stick or a number one, a line of counting. Living from this 'I', whatever we start to do, we calculate, we gather, subtract, multiply or divide, so one is the starting point, the one, 1, the 'I' who does all that.

Taking this basic picture of 'I' as a stick, if we are out in the forest and want to build a shelter we can gather sticks and lean them either together or against a tree (a bigger stick stuck in the ground) and then we have a construction. And it is the same with 'I' in the plural. If we lay the 'I's together, lean them against each other, then that collection of 'I am this' and 'I am that' or 'I believe this' or 'I believe that' makes up who we take ourselves to be, but if we remove the sticks one by one then there is no longer a construct which can stand. Even the 'I' that made the whole construction was like the tree – just another big stick or, in the case of our minds, another thought like all the other thoughts. Sticks. Functional units of counting or packets of fuel to be used. Again, functional.

All the 'I's together make up an illusion, an appearance, the sense of 'I'. It is, again, an accumulation, a collection of things which are counted, fuel blocks saved up, ideas of having power through collecting.

Collecting, accumulating and appearing
Power against
Protection from existence
Saving for a rainy day
When existence does not rain on you
Or reign over you and provide.

If I reduce myself to being a collection of ideas, I am no longer existential, and in denying my existence, my life, I of course deny existence. When I deny existence, existence cannot rain over me, or provide for me. I am restricted to a land of ideas, a barren land, a desert isolated from life. A fertile land is a land disturbed by weather systems, life and death, and the good farmer knows he must turn the soil and at times leave land fallow.

This collecting and calculating is a miscalculation made in a case of mistaken identity. When all that has been collected is removed, there is no error: then there is clarity, because life is not filtered through all the ideas we have collected and rejected. I say collected and rejected because we do not see and cannot consider that which we have rejected, but still it contributes to our misunderstanding and the distortion of vision as our perception will be full of holes.

What 'is' is seen as it is in totality, and only in this seeing can there be an action which is a response and which is also whole, a response of the individual being. A response which is whole and brings about wholeness: strange though it may sound, the response adds to wholeness. The response 'makes' the individual richer and deeper and more individual. The individual contains more, but does not contain in the way that they did when collecting. The individual sensing a greater totality becomes less. The boundaries of what they can collect are breached and they are flooded with what is. They become less and more is.

Through the stick metaphor we can see the functionality of 'I', the ego and the mind. We build a structure when a shelter is needed, but it is we who come and go into and out of the shelter: we don't need to carry the shelter with us. When it rains we might take cover, in the sun we seek shade and at night a place to sleep, but we do not live permanently in the shelter – that would be a prison – nor do we carry it with us and it definitely is not who we are. But a prison is what we turn the functionality of the mind into when we identify the mind and all its concepts and ideas to be who we are.

In the functional sense the construction is useful. The same with 'I' – it is functional, but we do not need to go on carrying it everywhere. Rather we can use it when we need it and put it down when its function is not needed.

In this way we can use it but remain clear it is not who we are. I the builder, I the driver, I the father, I the mother, I the son or the daughter, I the doctor and I the patient are all useful for appearances and functionality but are not the real 'I'.

Going back to the original analogy, let's take the word 'construction' as we applied it to 'I' or to sticks leaning against a tree. The dictionary definition of con- or col- as a prefix as in 'construct' or 'collect' means to join, with, together. So who does the joining and the collecting? The joiner joins all the elements of how we then appear to be as a structure, but the joiner is not found inside the structure. And when the shelter is dismantled, who is the one who remains?

Surface Tension

We use surface tension to make our reality stick together.

Self-enquiry, like hot water and soap, breaks the fatty film and the surface tension of our projected reality by breaking apart the illusion of who we think we are and the world this projects. The tensions are the differences we create, essentially the difference between 'I' and 'not I' which, if we examine it, is random.

Is air or space my space or your space? It appears as my space if I lay claim to it. And to breathe air is to make it my air if, again, I lay claim to it. But examine breath. Breath is a need of the body. That body is, again, a random or illusory idea of 'my body', because if any of us looked at a piece of our own skin or any part of the body under a microscope we would not recognise it as ours. So this idea of something being ours must be something other than recognising the body in the way we recognise a car or house. Perhaps it is a feeling, but again we all feel the same things: we feel emotions of anger, fear, happiness and sadness, we feel physically hot and cold, or we feel texture as rough or smooth.

But what is it, then, that makes the feeling 'mine' a unique and specific 'mine-ness'? As we all feel the same things, feeling by itself cannot be the declaration of person-hood, so perhaps it is the 'me-ness', because I cannot have mine, as in my feeling, without me. This 'me' only exists for you, so in a way it also does not exist, because when I am alone I am not me – I only say that to you or I may *think* that. 'Me' is only functional: it is a way of drawing imaginary lines, especially concerning possession. A car which is mine can become somebody else's if I sell it or if I die. Wives and husbands referred to as 'mine' can become someone else's 'property', so clearly our deepest and most precious things are not really ours. People even change their minds, so what happens to all 'their' opinions and beliefs? Exchanged, released, jettisoned? Who is released then – the belief or the person? And if the person is released, then who are they without their mind – or are they?

So we come back to: me only exists for you. If I am alone, I am 'I', or I am, or ... because words cannot touch this. Now *that* would be a good starting point. All these experiences I have of me and mine and differences can be seen to be built on 'I', the 'I' thought, and this seems to be where the tension starts. I am different: I experience all this but I am none of it. This is the root of separation. However, this can be the door to either separation or liberation. I experience all this but am none of it, which is separation. Or, I experience all of this and I am all of this, which is liberation. Or, I experience all this but am none of it, which is separation that is also liberation, because I also experience 'I' all the time and I admit that all my experience is not 'I', so 'I' is not who I am, so I am liberated from myself. Or, I experience all of this and I am all of this, which is liberation in the totality of life, so if there is liberation all of this is liberated as there is no longer a separate 'I' to be liberated. So stop the rave!

This is the simplicity that all experience but most people do not want to admit to. The idea that creates the separation is self-created. Before the idea arises, there is no difference. This idea 'I' is the one we think we are, which contains the collection of ideas given to us and adopted by us, also known as social custom. That self-creation causes the tension because this idea, not being who we are, needs to be created again and again, and this requires effort and protection. No wonder it is so hard to protect and nobody really succeeds: how can anyone protect something which does not exist? If you live like this you had better look out. Literally, when we live like this we have to look OUT, because it is the outside, society's customs, morals, fashions and trends, which calls the tune. But that is always changing and hence does not exist, in the same way that the sky does not really exist as it is also constantly changing. The word 'sky' exists, but does not signify anything other than that it is up there. Protecting something that nobody can define because it is changing is like being afraid to lose something you do not have but have convinced yourself you do have, and you keep it locked in a safe that you have never looked in.

Look inside yourself. Maybe what you are protecting does not exist. Well, don't take my word for it – go and take a look!

The tension is inherent, firstly in the holding and protecting, but also in looking away. How can something go on appearing to exist when it does not, except when the person who is experiencing it is not looking directly at the place where they expect to find it? This can only happen when the person is either looking away while professing to take a direct look, or when that person is not looking directly but looking indirectly. By looking indirectly, I mean taking hearsay or superstition as perception. Taking what is read, or what somebody has told them, as fact. Now a direct look will require a sharp mind, so it is better to sharpen our minds by clearing our heads of all the clutter that creates indirect experience.

The point is that the surface tension holding a soap bubble together is creating something whole, whereas the surface tension we experience is fighting against that wholeness and attempting to create separation where there is already wholeness. The bubble reflects the whole of the earth and sky on its surface. When the bubble bursts, the earth and sky are still here. We are consciousness and can reflect the earth and the sky or whatever surrounds us. You cannot burst consciousness. Try to deny that you exist! One way to create a reality over the top of what is here is to look away and pretend that what is presenting itself is not here, by limiting oneself to mind and holding a thought that something else is going on. That is like the soap bubble having a memory and floating thoughts, or the sky deciding it does not like the cloudy day but prefers the sunny day and projecting on its surface, its consciousness, the memory of that sunny day.

So 'I am' is the surface tension that either joins all together as a whole or divides and creates separation by becoming 'I am this' and holding apart all the rest, which it has decided it is not. Both are tension, and the way we use 'I' is our choice. So take note: the New Age dream of relaxation, returning to the womb, the enlightenment where you disappear and become a non-being, blank, a robot of God, is a dream. To be alive is tension – sorry dreamers! We use the tension to go on making our reality stick together. Our reality sticks with us as either our enemy or our friend, either as part of us or not, either as something we can accept or something we cannot or do not want to accept as our doing, and of which we are victims. Which means either something we go on stirring up because we fight it, or something we observe and accept, realise is in us and make peace with.

The surface is mental: it is where we hold the ideas and create the conflict, for creative or destructive purposes or just to play. Feeling is deeper. When we feel, we cannot hold these ideas and we start to join what appears divided. The outside becomes inside. The enemy becomes the familiar, who I recognise in myself because I am the enemy *and* the familiar, as both are in me. This is both joining and dissolving the forms created. They seem to be there because we see their surfaces, but beneath the surfaces the essence is revealed. The only way to see and experience this is to become that essence.

On Fear and Non-Definition

Fear of going in or Being is the realisation of our non-being. We sense we continue to exist beyond any thing, but this being beyond things is undefined and this touching on non-definition evokes fear for the individual. We are leaving definition as an object and entering the definitionless, but we still exist – in fact this is our nature. The trick is to adopt definition again, otherwise the world of definition crushes us, because we still live in this world. The world of definition floods into us, because we live in a world where the laws of nature do not allow a vacuum. The difference now is that the definitionless is our definition – it is what we are – and our doing is just that – doing – it is not how we define ourselves.

So now, rather than greeting another and asking, 'How are you?' we could accelerate the evolution of humankind by simply changing this to, 'Who are you?' This may be a little strange to begin with, but in the long term extremely beneficial and enlightening. Because 'how' always refers to a doing, as in, 'How are you doing?' it does not refer to the being of a person. So every time this, 'How are you?' is repeated as a ritual it deepens the conditioning and the identification of a doer. Whereas, 'Who are you?' goes straight to being, as it asks, 'Who are you being?' Now any doers instantly disappear.

What a wholesome ritual for those who care about realisation, where fellow travellers ask each other, 'Who are you being?' If a person is being themselves, meaning there is nothing *but* being, then an answer is not required, not even a polite gesture, whereas in the event that a definitionless being has been practising the bad habit of trying to be somebody, then the question will be quite amusing. I mean, if we can see we are trying to be that which we are not, what a celebration and what a relief, and the question may be answered as follows: 'Oh, I was being ...' You just fill in the gap, move in and move on.

You may ask how, then, do we live in this world where definitions are a part of daily life? To this I say that, from being definitionless, the required definition will appear without fail. The required definition is a response and is always the right one, because we are present, aware, and part of our surroundings. In fact being and response are just extensions of our surroundings. There is a stone in your glove; when you have dealt with it by removing it, you can return to the definitionless.

Applying the Mind or the Right Bus for the Destination

For the mind to think it is useless is taboo. In thinking it is useless, the mind grabs at any thought so that it can become the doer and feel useful again. This grabbing at thoughts is like standing at a bus stop in a strange town where you want to go to the station. Not knowing which bus to take and not wanting to stand around, looking lost and useless, you take every bus that comes along and end up going everywhere. In the mind, this fear of being useless can drive us to jump on any thought and go anywhere, everywhere, all the time. On the other hand, if we don't get muddled by emotions, we can apply our minds, see where we are and where we want to go and get the information to bridge the gap. Now informed, we apply those thoughts and go to our destination, the station.

Uncovering Feeling-Being

We empower thoughts and give them life until they appear to have a life of their own. When we stop giving the thoughts energy, they settle. While we give thoughts our life energy, they grow into worlds, and we believe certain thoughts are who we are and certain thoughts are not who we are. Then we have likes and dislikes, or things we desire and things we resist. When we can allow thoughts to just be and allow emotions to just be, then they settle, and a feeling arises that was being covered by the thoughts and emotions. This is not something we like or dislike; it is the feeling of being, which is natural and effortless.

Identification Is the Nature of 'I'

The ego's tendency to escape and not be seen is the ego's expression of its ambivalence and the realisation that what it has, and is, is not real. Really it just appears to escape, to always be just leaving. It is never the one to stand up. Because of this illusory performance of the ego, only ever being seen as a glimpse, in the act of disappearing, it is necessary to hold on to the individual 'I' in the act of awareness sitting practice. Normally, the 'I' falls into what is being watched and falls asleep, and this leads to deeper identification. Don't be so concerned about the silence and the subsiding phenomena and don't be fooled by this disappearance happening. Instead wait, and deliberately keep the separation between the observer you call 'I', you the subject, and that which is observed, the object. Allow the dance between them. In this movement, 'I' falls into the Real in a natural motion, which is not a motion on the part of the individual but rather a realisation of what is Real and that the subject and the object have the same root. There is no question of movement or choice because there is nothing else but the Real, and the 'I' identifies with that, as identification is its nature. Another way to see it is that by doing this we experience the object and the subject together.

'I' is just an abbreviation for identification.

Summary

Hold the 'I' as a separate observer until there is nothing from which to separate and observe, and then be That, identify with That.

There's a Natural Gain

There's a natural gain, investing in
The rest is, out sourcing
That direction, the resulting disconnection
No interest, no one involved
In-vest, know the true interest.

PART 5

The Power of the Word and Voice – Poems

The IN-Word Movement

The poems in this section are best read aloud, and then the real can be discovered. All that is real is happening now.

In dancing, the real dance is an inner dance. The more the body is just allowed to be, the more the dancer moves inward and the less the body is interfered with, until the body is just responding and the one who before was busy being the dancer is now just aware of dancing.

If music is such a powerful medium of expression, which touches people and brings them to certain deeper feelings, then without a doubt the voice of the individual speaking and hearing one's own voice must be much more powerful phenomena. The intimacy of each individual's voice carries such potential and richness to be experienced that the use of it should not be ignored.

I suggest the poems be read aloud so the reader can hear their own voice. Repeat the poems and continue to listen and watch. Sound reveals the context, silence. If we listen to a sound and follow its fading, we follow our perception back to source. In music, especially when it is studio orientated, that seems for me to be the attraction of the use of echo. When the echo is repeating and fading, the listener travels both horizontally in time and vertically inward to the place where the sound disappears. So experiment with your voice, experiment on consecutive days and notice what changes there are. As with all parts of the book, play with the content and make it yours.

Deep

Take 'deep', the thought, inside. Hold it and digest it.
This will reveal to you what deep IS.

Depth is the current. Picture a river, the surface is moving as are the interior deeper levels of the river. You can just dip your finger into the surface and feel the current flowing, but the real current is deeper. The real current is in the depth.

At the surface the current is mixed with our ideas. Actually our 'I' is the interface, and the deeper we go into the river the stronger is the current and the weaker are our ideas and hence the weaker is the 'I', until there is no difference between the 'I' and the current. Now that is deep. 'I' always has ideas of how life should be, but when 'I' is merged with that which is, then everything is experienced in its depth, in reality not as separate. Now I am real and what I experience is real, as one, with no interference of mind, ideas and beliefs.

Do we really know the meaning of words? Have we tasted words and got behind the ideas which they are encased in? Have we let them melt in our mouths like the soft centre of a hard-boiled sweet? Have we ourselves melted enough to let them really speak to us beyond the meaning we think and allocate to them, beyond the idea that we are using them? Consider that words may be using us; we just need to allow ourselves to be used. We are naturally attracted to certain words and language. Scientific language, poetic language, street language, slang and dialect. Words have been travelling for so long and they do carry power. How can a Zen practitioner working with Mu (an answer given by Zen Master Joshu in thirteenth century China to a monk's question as to whether a dog has Buddha nature) come to realise that which the Master realised all those years ago? Anything will do where the mind is focused and has to drop itself, going beyond its idea that it knows the answer. Tone and expression also carry power, as in Mu, Aum, Allah Hoo or Yaa-Hoo!

Try the method above with other words. Zen people who work with koans will at times do this as they struggle with their koan. They will imbibe, digest, take in, feel and become the words or the anecdote and then they will know the meaning. Mother, sky, earth, love, ocean, silence. Children know this. Actors who experiment with different expressive deliveries of their lines, singing them, crying them, raging them, serenading a lover with them as a technique for learning them will know, as will anybody who has eaten poetry, turned it over in their mouth allowing the membranes of the mouth, the throat and vocal chords, the ears and head, the heart, the respiratory muscles and all the cells of the body to experience what the words hold. One word can be a universe; taste the essential in that particular form.

Each of Us a Prayer

Each of us a prayer
Each of us a psalm
Each of us a koan

Each of us the answer
Asking the question

Praying
Psalming
Koaning.

Here Before and Arriving With ...

It IS NOT
Staring you in your face
It is IN your face staring
It is IN your breath breathing
It is IN your heart beating
Closer than ...

It was here before, and it arrives with ... the breath.

Then We Will See

Kidnap thoughts and take them with you to the Lord
Then we will see
Take life the in breath out to no breath
Then we will see.

BE – The Low Lord

BELOW the being that is up, in control and has the experience of a separated self is a depression, a sadness, a softness and finally a not-being. Not-Being not being in control, there is an inter-dependency. It is a connectedness.

It is below I move, down from doing, controlling and knowing-about into being connected-with. It is communication with another if needed, but basically it is in connection and communication, full and stop.

'I' doesn't like this because, in this below, 'I' feels robbed and powerless. 'I' feels like it has given over, given away to a lesser power. 'I' misses the buzz, the drug of power and doing and being in control.

But down below, the patient one, in the foundation, waited. How low can I go? Where is this deeper trough? On what does all this rest?

The Low Lord.

Welcome or Illcome

If we dis ease
We are diseased
If we are ease
We can be ill or well
What the hell
Welcome or illcome
But no disrespect

Look again

If we dis ease
We are diseased
If we are ease
We can be
Ill or well
What the hell
Welcome or illcome
But no disrespect

Look
Again

If we dis ease
We are diseased

Welcome or illcome
If we are ease
We can be ill or well
Whatever the hell
Welcome or illcome
But no disrespect

Look
A gain.

Water's Poem

Letting settle
Sitting
Closing eyes
Water thinks
It is an ocean
Somewhere
Though here
In a glass

All stirred up
In motion
Thinks water
'I'm a storm'

Sitting, settling
Closing eyes
Falling
Seeing

Better I be broken
Than dream of oceans
Better spilt, splashed, dashed
Washing you and I
Down.

Spring

Birdsong is pulling my mouth to smile.

The Sun

The sun is not out
And it does not shout
It is bathing itself from the inside.

Candle Flame

The candle flame retains its goal, its intention, its direction
It knows where home is
It reaches and rises to its highest
In draughts it sways, then returns to its inner aim
Knowing

Light is not its concern.

Illuminating

Holding a lighted match
Seeing it is fading
Stop any movement
Tilt its angle down
Illuminating

Losing hold of the senses
Emotional and defensive
Stop mind and tongue
Tilt attention down
Illuminating.

If We Want To Be Light

If we want to be light we have to let go. When we let go of what we
are carrying we do become LIGHT.

No Wonder

When we don't look
It is no wonder
We can't see

When we can't be
It is no wonder
That we can't do

When we confuse doing for being
And appearing for seeing

So it all appears

No wonder
No wonder.

The Riverbed or Lie Down and Wake Up

Thoughts run, it does not move
Riverbed stones become smooth
River flows, stones do nothing
One thought moving, a smooth mind.

We Have Time or Time Has Us

We either have time or time has us
When we have no time, time has us completely
Having time we forget time.

Winter in Worthing

Snow on the beach
Blue sky
No leaves on the trees
Butterfly.

By Helen and Cyrus

Picking Apples

Circling the tree
Each new angle brings new apples
Sometimes, surprisingly

Aiming for one goal, new apples are sighted
Circling, circling
All apples are seen

Ten per cent for the birds and insects
Time for supper.

The Off-Centre Forward

(One for the footballers and fans thereof)

When I am outside
Of myself
I am offside
I think
I am part of the game
But have set myself apart
Anything I do from here
Is short-lived till the whistle blows.

I have no team
Or opposition
I – have – no – position
I am not in the vision
I've set myself apart
Till the whistle blows
And with a start
I wake up.

The Whole Is Peace

The whole is peace
The piece is whole
Piece has an i
Peace has an a

A, B, C

A is the first
I comes later

Yes you write
But first comes the paper.

There's a Natural Gain

There's a natural gain, investing in
The rest is, out sourcing
That direction, the resulting disconnection
No interest, no one involved
In-vest, know the true interest.

Begin

The word begin, see
First it says be

Always beginning we are
Thinking to have gone so far

Our overnight stay
Begins again today

Begin again we
No again be.

I, Be, See

If you were not as I, Being
There would be no Seeing
Literacy starts with ABC
Before these comes I, Be, See
THAT as I, to Be and See
IS the One in all three.

The Proof

Proof is proof
This is not I

Proof is proofed
Subtle defence
And the fence limits
Proofed against.

Justify

To justify myself
Is to 'just if I' myself
When I am I
I am
No justs or ifs or buts or plans.

Thinking

Thinking, sifting, sorting, judging

Apart

A part judging the Whole.

Where's the Question?

(Read the following lines aloud, progressively lowering your voice until you are intoning it silently.)

Where's the question?
Where's the question?
Where's the question?

It's You You See

The one who sees is in the middle
It is you, the seer
See?

The one who sees is in the distance, out there
It is you, the seer
See?

The in, the out, all around about
It's you you see
You see?

It's a Coming Around Round Thing

All that is forgotten
Has previously been got
So don't worry
It's a come around thing
And it's round becoming

Still still still.

Do Not Wipe Your Feet

DO NOT wipe
your feet
It's enlightenment
you've stepped in

DO NOT
wipe your feet
It's enlightenment

YOU have stepped IN.

I Am Now And ...

I am not the truth, you are
You are not the truth, we are
We are not the truth, truth is
Truth is not the truth
Now is
I am now
And ...

(Repeat until ...)

All These Selves

All these selves
Are all themselves
Who have no Self
While speaking
For themselves.

I Live at House I

I live at house I
I am inside
But I don't find me there.

All Are Leaning In

The poet leans on words
The cook on food
The dancer leans on the body
And all are leaning in.

Flooding and Streaming

Awareness is ecstasy, is love, is peace
It flows, going nowhere
Longing without longing, it is eternally long, eternal
It is attention and appreciation
It greets, greeting nobody, knowing itself in all forms
It loves without creating another, as it is love
It pours but does not empty, knowing no beginning or end.

The Secret

The secret is secreting
God is leaking.

Spirituality (18)

Admit

We want our spirituality
Delivered safely, seriously
We dress it up as learning
Consume it and call it spirit

We learn, but little touches or changes us
We won't admit we're being entertained
So we dress it up
Better would be to get down

In sex, it involves those involved
The more present one is, the more's experienced

In drinking spirit, at least the drinker gets drunk
And learns where the false source is
Headaches can be avoided
Mind ache is hard to locate

Words by nature spin
We won't catch the source in
Till we drop
Down

Submit.

Everything

Everything is out
Even in is out
Out of the starting point
See the point

Everything is empty
Of itself and so full
Every thing's got a name
But not one that can remain.

About the Author

Cyrus Bruton was born in England in 1960. He is a spiritual teacher who has travelled extensively, spending prolonged periods of time in India in the 1980s and 1990s. He was initiated into neo-sannyas by Osho (Bhagwan Shree Rajneesh) in 1983. He has celebrated, lived, worked and meditated in communes internationally, trained in bodywork and dance, and participated in the Therapist Training programme at the Osho Humaniversity in Holland with Veeresh Denny Yuson-Sanchez. In 1997 he came into contact with Anamo (Mikaire), and then spent the next twelve years in Mikaire's teaching. He has been sharing Satsang since 1999. He has completed the Avatar materials and is a certified Holotropic Breathwork facilitator. Presently, Cyrus lives, works and teaches in Berlin with his beloved, a growing community of fellow travellers and two exquisite cats. He shares Satsang and offers retreats and Holotropic Breathwork.